Date Due

Oct 2			
Oct 11 80			
Fe 28'81			
Ja 17'83			
Oct 9 84			
Jan 26 '85			
Feb 11			
Fe 25 85			
Mr 16 85			
NOV 13			
JUL 8			

BIG TIMBER   BIG MEN

BIG TIMBER BIG MEN

Carol J. Lind

ISBN 0−88839−020−3
Copyright © 1978 Carol J. Lind

Cataloging in Publication Data

Lind, Carol J.
Big timber, big men

Bibliography: p.
Includes index.
ISBN 0-88839-020-3

1. Logging—United States—History.
2. Logging—Canada—History. I. Title.
SD538.2.A1L55 338.1'7'49820973 C78-002094-4

Published simultaneously in Canada and the United States by:

HANCOCK HOUSE PUBLISHERS LTD.
3215 Island View Road SAANICHTON, B.C. V0S 1M0

HANCOCK HOUSE PUBLISHERS INC.
12008 1st Avenue South SEATTLE, WA. 98168

Contents

Dedication

Without the aid of my father, John E. Lind, who brought home the first logging pictures and loggers' folklore, this book would not have been possible. This is also in appreciation of my mother, Cora.

Acknowledgements

Aberdeen City Library
Aberdeen, Washington

British Columbia Provincial Archives
Victoria, British Columbia

Everett Public Library
Everett, Washington

Custom Photo Service
Littlerock, Washington

Forest Service
Government of British Columbia

Jones Photo Company
Aberdeen, Washington

Minnesota Historical Society
St. Paul, Minnesota

Oregon Historical Society
Portland, Oregon

Provincial Archives of New Brunswick
Fredericton, New Brunswick

Seattle Historical Society
Seattle, Washington

Tacoma Public Library
Tacoma, Washington

Tumwater City Library
Tumwater, Washington

Vancouver Public Library
Vancouver, British Columbia

Washington State Historical Society
Tacoma, Washington

Washington State Library
Olympia, Washington

Weyerhaeuser Archives
Tacoma, Washington

7

8

Timber stands so thick that sunlight trickled to the forest floor between massive boughs. Trees so tall the first branch was eighty feet above the ground.

Foreword

This book is not a definitive study of the logging industry. It would take a series of volumes and the contribution of many historians to accomplish that purpose. Rather *BIG TIMBER! BIG MEN!* is a series of events.

Nor should one conclude from the chapters pertaining to the labor movement that all logging companies were bad. For every company against the fledgling unions was another which provided medical care and emergency methods to transport the injured out of the woods to company hospitals—such as the one provided by Walter M. Reed of Simpson Timber, McCleary, Washington; clean bunk houses, even family apartment buildings such as provided by Polson Logging Company, Montesano, Washington; European trained chefs—such as imported from the New York Waldorf Astoria by the Schafer Brothers of Upper Satsop, Washington, to cook for their loggers; weekend trips into town for loggers and their families—such as provided by Simon Benson Logging Company; company safe deposit vaults—such as provided by Pope and Talbot of Port Gamble, Washington (which company's houses resemble a New England village); modern management techniques—early used by the James Logging Company of Cowichan, British Columbia.

Nor were all the loggers as a group entirely made up of men anxious to get drunk on those twice-a-year holidays. Those who were not part of the get-drunk-and-spend-your-pay crowd were usually loners or went home to visit their families. For some, being a logger was a chosen way of life; they would have it no other way. But it was a hard life, and liquor softened sharp edges of grim reality. For others, there was no other opportunity; thus, discontent.

9

Because some logging operations were so bad, so inefficient, so unfeeling toward their workers, there was a rallying to the cry of unionism. The union movement came about at a time of tremendous social unrest. There had been much abuse by "plutocrats" in Eastern sweatshops, and the importation of cheap labor to work in unsafe conditions created a need for workers to band together into unions. The early union organizers recognized that in numbers there was strength. This distrust of management carried over into the forest industry and was shared by the workers—certainly not without reason. At this time, the anchors that held society steady were wrenched free by the Great War—a war few people could understand. A complete social order of European aristocracy had been overthrown. A Russian czar and his family were shot in a far-off basement. It was a time adrift. It was a time of distrust. It was, for them, the worst of times for civilized guidelines lacked meaning. Men cast about for better ways to live, while extremists stood on soapboxes and challenged their governments to do better. If it was over-reaction by the powerful fearing a Russian Revolution was imminent in North America, it was no less an over-reaction by those who feared anyone of independent thought.

Each event at the moment of happening has a purpose and meaning, often not to be revealed for years.

Yet it is just as wrong to say the logging companies were the culprits. There was, after all, extremism on both sides. What happened in those years was as complicated, as varied, as murky in motives as the people involved. It happened. It is part of documented history. It is the stuff of which legends are made. Upon those foundations a new lumber industry was built.

Those companies which opposed change in any form disappeared, unable to compete. Those which survived had already been changing or were ahead of change—were even innovators. Those that started their logging complexes in the aftermath learned from the experiences of those that did not survive. They recognized that change is constant; change is the one business rule that does not change.

BIG TIMBER! BIG MEN! is about an industry in change, why it was changing and those factors which forced the industry to change more rapidly when it appeared reluctant to do so. While it empathizes with the pursuit of workers to force change, it is no less a tribute to those companies which urged change.

Logging camp bunkhouse in Minnesota.

1

Migration West

Hell-bent for the next "tall and uncut" and hanging onto the Devil's coat-tails of wilderness the loggers ran ahead of civilization. In their wake they left stumps for John Farmer. The lumbermen had put "daylight into the swamp" of Pennsylvania—which had been the greatest lumber-producing state before the Civil War—and Maine by 1885.

They moved northwest into the Lake States, in particular to the Saginaw Valley of Michigan. Joining the American lumberjacks were the "shanty-boys" from the Canadian provinces of Nova Scotia and Quebec. The Canadian shanty-boys were anxiously welcomed for they were known to be the best "river pigs" around when it came to wild river drives—and the Lake States heavily employed the river drive to get their logs to market. Along the twenty-mile stretch on the banks of the Saginaw were sawmills with stacks of drying lumber, all competing mightily "to get in and cut out." The white "cork" pine and the Norway "red" pine carpeted the rivers in a head-long rush to Au Sable, Thunder Bay, Cheboygan, Maistee and Muskegon lumbering centers.

Logging in the Michigan pineries was a rough affair done only in the winter when the ground was frozen solid. The camps were temporary. One large bunk shanty served all the men. A "camboose"—a square of raised earth in the center of the shanty floor where a fire was maintained—was both heat and light. Smoke escaped through a hole in the roof. The bough-mattress bunks were built to accomodate twenty or thirty men. They slept in a row with their heads to the wall and feet toward the fire. All shared a common blanket.

Grabbing a quick breakfast about three o'clock in the morning which they had usually prepared themselves, the "shanty-boys" bundled in black woolen underwear, two woolen shirts, dirt-stiff

13

Loggers' Song
(Year: 1906)

Long haired preachers come out every night
Try to tell you what's wrong and what's right;
But when asked how 'bout something to eat
They will answer with voices so sweet;
You will eat, bye and bye
In that glorious land above the sky;
Work and pray, live on hay,
You'll get pie in the sky when you die.

Work could be found among the Minneapolis, Minnesota, Bridge Square employment bureaus in 1908.

Minnesota Historical Society.

14

They came to a new country where they worked hard at back-breaking jobs.

pants, double socks, caulk boots, and plaid mackinaws. They filed into the woods where the trees were felled, limbed, bucked into logs, then skidded to loading landings by teams of either oxen or horse. The loads were built up on bob-sleds—better known as sleighs—often as much as twelve feet wide. It was the Canadian "shanty-boys" who contributed the skidway to logging in Minnesota. Contrary to popular opinion, this did not come from Maine. The sled roads had been prepared while the loggers slept in the shanty. A night crew drove water sprinklers over the roads during the freezing hours, building a slick road that easily skidded the sleighs to "banking grounds" or "rollways" on the steep banks of the rivers.

When the spring thaw came and freshets poured wildly through the rising channels, the logs were released. The dangerous river drive to the sawmills had begun. Caught up in the swift current the logs tumbled through the boulder strewn, crooked rivers, always threatening with a log jam.

Logs jam a shallow river.

Three crews usually worked on the typical log drives—sometimes two crews were enough. Usually in the vanguard were the "huskies" who were young and agile. This driving crew would be spread along the streams for ten or fifteen miles. They urged the logs along, keeping them out of shoal water, steering them into inlets and pockets and keeping them in the mainstream. The next group of huskies was the jam crew. Any part of the river drive was dangerous, but they had the most dangerous job of all. They had to make certain the logs did not pile into a jam. If a jam did occur, they had to dynamite it free. The timing of the explosion might not blow as intended; bits of debris could maim or kill, or the destructive force of the backed-up waters would suck them under.

This crew easily flea-hopped from log-to-log during the drive; occasionally somebody did slip. The songs of the North Woods loggers are heavily versed with "poor, drowned shanty-boys," such as the old ballad, *The Jam on Gerry's Rocks.*

1.
You shanty-boys, you drivers, come list while
    I relate
Concerning a young riverman and his
    untimely fate.
Concerning a young riverman so manly,
    true and brave—
It was on the jam on Gerry's rocks that he met
    his watery grave.

2.
It was on a Sunday morning as quick as you
    will hear.
Our saw logs piled up mountains high, we
    could not keep them clear,
Till our foreman said, "Turn out, brave boys,
    with hearts we'll avoid all fear.
We'll break the jam on Gerry's rocks and for
    Eganstown we'll steer."

3.
Some of them went willingly, while others
    they hung back.
For to break a jam on Sunday they did not
    think it right,
Till six of our Canadian boys did volunteer to
    go
For to break the jam on Gerry's rocks with
    their foreman, young Monroe.

4.
They had not rolled off many logs when they
    heard the clear voice say:
"I'd have you boys be on your guard, this jam
    will soon give way."
Those words were scarcely spoken when the
    jam did break and go
And carried off those six brave youths and
    their foreman, young Monroe.

5.
The rest of those shanty-boys those sad
    tidings came to hear,
In search of the drowned bodies down the
    river they did steer,
Till one of those poor bodies to their sad grief
    and woe
All bruised and mangled by the rocks lay the
    head of young Monroe.

6.
They raised him from his watery grave,
    combed back his coal black hair.
There was one fair form amongst them whose
    cries would rend the air:
There was one fair form amongst them, a girl
    from Saginaw town;
Her moans and sighs would rend the skies for
    her true love that was drowned.

7.
Poor Clara did not survive long through her
  sad grief and woe.
Poor Clara did not survive long through her
  sad grief and woe.
It was in about three weeks after that she was
  called to go,
And her last request was granted, to be laid
  by young Monroe.

8.
So come all of you bold shanty-boys, I'd have
  you call and see
A little mound by the river bend where stands
  a hemlock tree,
And the shanty-boys cut the woods all down,
  two lovers there lie low;
There lies Miss Clara Verner and her true
  love, young Monroe.

The veterans or true "river pigs" were in rear crew. They had to "sack out the shallows" where logs drifted into shallow water or against stream banks. With peaveys and sweat this largely Canadian and Maine-staters crew rolled the twisting logs into the main stream. As they waded through the shallows, sand from the churned river bed would sloush up over their boot-tops, seeping down to sandpaper the flesh. For these men, "Squeak Heel" or sore feet was an occupational hazard which they tended to when night came and they bedded down on the damp shore. Camping for the "river pigs" was the most primitive type imaginable.

It was no wonder that at the end of the drive, the men turned to drink, tearing the raw lumber towns apart in their anger and frustration. Hard on the lumberjack's heels had come the saloons and the brothels. For a brief time they were free men abiding no law except their own. No town clown dared to interfere when the lumberjacks threw each other through a saloon window . . . or a wall. While the lumberjacks considered it unethical, sometimes the temper overruled reason. On occasion when a man was down, the winner stomped on his belly, chest and face with steel-spiked boots, permanently imprinting him with "logger's smallpox."

As fate would have it, those establishments which catered to the lumberjack became high-hat by putting up signs, "Caulked Boots Not Allowed Here." Hotels nailed up "Take Off Your Boots Before Retiring." The swamp angels—prostitutes—even wanted the lumberjacks to take baths first. Waves of moralist thinking closed down the chippy joints, which just as quickly reopened.

Working from river boats peaveymen guide logs in a drive to the market.

It was to be expected. The farmers came to claim the logged-off land which land speculators offered at cheap prices—the farmers were yet to learn the sandy loam was fit for little else than growing timber. In their eagerness to farm, the settlers cleared away slash and what timber remained with fires, destroying the seed trees and burning the life out of the forest soil. With the farmers came proper women, children, preachers, storekeepers and assorted moralists who talked against the bad influence of the heathen lumberjacks and their wanton painted women. There was talk the blood and guts fights had to cease. Decent folk couldn't understand men who ripped into booze, battle and bawds—the trinity of the lumberjack.

Logging camp messhall in Wisconin.

A cookhouse in Eastern Canada.

An eastern Canada log shute was the prototype for western sawmills.

In eastern Canada, horsepower and human muscle power kept the mills running.

Lumberjack . . . logger . . . hard, lusty fighting men who were a distinct breed. They were the first pioneers too light-footed to battle a constant living from the land. They cleared the land for those who followed. In those early years they ravished the land. That was their job and when they finished their job it was time to move on.

To be a lumberjack was survival of the fittest. They had survived Canadian and New England winters of "forty below," wild river drives of logs that twisted on rapid currents in the Lake States, the red-light districts . . . and each other.

One day the lumberjack looked around and saw the forests were gone. Lumber production was down. Towns had mushroomed around him. The whiskey was weak—the 110 proof they preferred was served less often. The fancy women objected to a man who hadn't bathed in six months, or longer, if ever. Holy Old Mackinaw, Civilization had caught up with them again. If they stayed civilization would kill them.

By the blue-eyed, bandy-legged, jumped-up old whistlin' Jesus H. Mackinaw Christ, it was time to haul out over the hump where another forest of piney wood waited for the axe. That meant the West Coast in general and the Pacific Northwest in particular.

The last large log drive in the Lake States was on the Menominee River in 1910. The migration west had begun twenty years earlier. A depression struck the country in the early 1890s. A number of the Saginaw mills closed down, never to open again. Once twenty-five million acres of pine had carpeted Michigan's sandy plains. Now it was mainly cutovers being torched by the farmers. The logger had fanned from Michigan to Wisconsin to Minnesota, always followed by the saloon owners, the swamp angels and eventually the farmer. The forest devastation was repeated leaving desolation and abandonment—even by the farmer who could grow nothing in the forest soil.

Some logging companies moved their logging operations lock, stock, barrel and crew. The trip by train proved boring to the restless loggers who couldn't abide sitting. Entertainment had to be devised. So the loggers howled back at the coyotes, then at each other. The train grew stuffy, even rank; it was easier to kick out a window than to open it. For really proper ventilation, they tore the doors off hinges. Train crews who had been shot at in one form or another by marauding Indians, mean closed-eyed outlaws and other assorted sissies had never seen the like of the loggers. Nor did they want to again.

Hearing what had happened to the trains, the sea captains had prepared for an interesting voyage. While not softies themselves, they were averse to loggers kicking out the sides of their ships. They filled their holds with the strongest 110 proof whiskey they could find. Quantity was more important than quality for the loggers drank everything from clear grain alcohol to canned heat, including the ship's turpentine.

Unhappily, the bawds left behind found themselves without free-spending customers. The civilized men were gawd-almighty tight with the dollar. The cut-over woods were ominously quiet. Logging camps were empty; buildings were left to rot. Sawmill whistles no longer blew. The howls of the lumberjacks and fists banging on brothel doors had ceased. In the meantime the swamp angels sat around and waited. They didn't wait long. Some of them packed their pink brocade corsets and followed the loggers West.

The river drivers of 1902, ate dinner on the river bank.

Among the loggers were many who played musical instruments.

Minnesota Historical Society.

Minnesota Historical Society.

22

Canadian loggers pose against a spruce, with a diameter of ten feet.

2

The West Coast

Along the west coast of the North American continent the Spanish had come and were summarily routed by the Americans. The Russians came for a time, but found it unprofitable, quickly selling Alaska to the Americans and firmly believing—at the time—they got the best of the deal. Worried about French domination, the British sent Hudson's Bay Company factors to secure their colonial outpost. For different reasons, the Eastern strangers slowly headed west.

Silently greeting them along the coastal land from Northern California up into what would become British Columbia were the Indians . . . and the trees. Gigantic trees that blocked out the sun. Trees with a girth unlike anything seen before.

The first recorded interest in the trees was by Captain James Cook in 1778 who ordered his sailors to replace the rotting masts of their ships with Douglas fir cut in Nootka Sound. Never before had a single tree been used for an entire mast. Previously two trees were needed to be spliced together permitting tall masts. The single masts stirred an interest in England . . . but this Colonial possession was so far away from any market.

So the trees in Canada were treated the same as in the United States: a nuisance to be cleared away so the land could be farmed. The trees provided material for shelter—nothing more.

Capt. James Cook.

23

What brought men West in the early years was fur to sell in the China market. Soon the Hudson's Bay Company had outposts in Western Canada and the Pacific Northwest. Astoria, Oregon, became the outpost for the fur trade among the Americans. Between the Americans and British developed a territorial rivalry.

Although primarily interested in fur and even gold, the British factors knew something useful could be made of the trees besides burning them to clear land. In 1847 sample spars were found to be superior to those from the Baltic, yet little interest was shown. The British were more concerned about the Americans who had been moving west since the Louisiana Purchase. American pioneers were settling on farm land in Oregon territory, making the British factors uneasy. In some areas, such as on San Juan Island, American and British settlers were living side by side which created a problem as to which government actually had a claim to the territory.

Into this casual tolerance that existed among the American and British settlers came Captain Brotchee. On an earlier expedition, Brotchee had recognized the monetary value of the standing timber. With backing from London businessmen, he secured licenses from the Admiralty and Hudson's Bay Company which allowed him to cut spars on Vancouver Island. Somehow, Brotchee got his directions confused when he excitedly returned to cut timber. He did not log on Vancouver Island. Instead, he started his operation near New Dungeness in Puget Sound— which happened to be on the American side. Why Brotchee didn't know he was not on an island only he could say but he apparently did not choose to explain. When the American customs officers in Astoria heard about the logging operation, they hot-footed it to the scene of the crime and promptly seized Brotchee's ship, the *Albion*. This was considered somewhat un-neighborly. But being civilized, the British protested in polite diplomatic correspondence that was exchanged for two years. Eventually the American courts paid the owners of the vessel $20,000.

British Columbia Forest Service

Lumber ships, 1902.

24

In the meantime, Brotchee had retreated to northern Vancouver Island. Employing Indians to cut spars, Brotchee invested all his money in the venture. After the spars were cut, he sought transportation to market. There were no ships available. Even though the Rear-Admiral in command of the Pacific Squadron and chief British factor Governor Douglas joined Brotchee in his entreaties to the Admiralty in London to provide ships, all requests fell on deaf ears. Brotchee lost all his money and the spars decayed on the beach. This first lumber export attempt in British Columbia was a precedent for the next four decades.

During Brotchee's unsuccessful bid to exploit British Columbia's standing timber, the Americans had been actively engaged in the lumber trade along the East Coast. Driven west by a dwindling timber supply and economic woes, the men who operated logging camps and sawmills already had the experience and the capital, and the waiting markets were gathering in San Francisco. Gold had been discovered in California. The golden catalyst that lured men by the thousands was about to make the Puget Sound mills whine in lumber production. The gold hunters were breaking trail for civilization. Towns would be built, towns that needed lumber. Some of the lumber would come from the California forests—but almost everyone in California was panning for gold. However, some lumber men had joined, often through marriage, with the great shipping families of the New England states. These businessmen envisioned more markets opening up. To the north of them in Oregon and Washington stood all the timber they desired. Briefly, they considered British Columbia. Shrugging their shoulders, they decided business with British Columbia officials was next to impossible, so they invested in American points of production.

Two men and a "misery whip."

25

Why was the timber wealth of British Columbia so ignored?

- It was remote—but then so was the Oregon territory.

- It lacked markets. In other words, it lacked businessmen with lumber contacts.

- It lacked transportation such as ships. The British ships in the waters around British Columbia were mainly military. Private ship-owners were reluctant to gamble on an untested product.

- Its timber regulations kept out the very men who could have developed the timber economy. In 1854 the Legislative Council of Vancouver passed several timber regulations, the most important being "no person not being subject to Her Majesty the Queen and resident of Vancouver's Island shall cut timber on public lands." This was a protective measure to insure British interests against the enterprising Americans who looked covetously at the great stands of timber north of the border. It had been the British officials' bitter experience that when one American moved in, others followed and they had an uncanny knack of soon possessing both legally and illegally what they wanted. Unfortunately, this regulation also kept out the very men who had the most experience in logging operations and lumber markets. Perhaps the regulation could have been written to allow the importing of technology—possibly the officials didn't trust the American "adventurers" who had all the skill of snake-oil pitchmen.

- Despite the urgings of senior servants, The Hudson's Bay Company seemed to discourage opening the country to commerce and settlers.

- There was also the obstacle of rank, class and connections. In England, no matter how wealthy one is, it is the blood that counts. English customs had been transported to British Columbia for the officials were usually the sons of the upper-crust. Ability meant nothing. Name meant everything. Americans had no time for such social distinctions; to them, business was business no matter who they dealt with. In England, business was trade and not for the likes of gentleman. The English officials who felt the only proper calling for their class was politics or the military distained business. To many of them, British Columbia was simply another outpost in their careers. They did not intend to stay.

The Americans couldn't understand this attitude—nor did they try. There was money to be made and jawboning with English officials in British Columbia who threw out roadblocks was simply a waste of time. While Governor Douglas did not share the same opinion of his countrymen, he was, after all only the Governor of British Columbia. As in America, that didn't mean those of influence would listen to the Governor.

So the Americans accepted the closed door policy and seized the lumber markets. The Reciprocity Treaty of 1854 that was signed

Canadian loggers falling a Douglas fir.

26

between the British North American Colonies and the United States was to encourage trade for British Columbia in the California market. Well, it did . . . up to a point. The problem was, the Americans already had the sawmills churning out wood, had ships speeding between points of production and delivery, and could deliver. The fledgling lumber men in British Columbia had a late start and were finding it almost impossible to compete.

British Columbia lumbering hit peaks and valleys, never maintaining a steady course that encouraged the necessary financial backers. Besides, most financial backers in the lumber industry were American and they were effectively locked out of British Columbia.

During the California gold rush Captain Walter C. Grant settled on Vancouver Island with the intent of operating a sawmill. He lacked lumber experience. He also failed.

The Muir family acquired Grant's mill. They were among the early few to be successful. By 1878 they were exporting piles and spares to San Francisco, Australia, China, South America and England. The American Civil War had certainly played a part in their success, for competition from below the border greatly decreased. After the American Civil War, there was a crying need for lumber. The South had to be rebuilt, the American west was opening up, railroads were about to cross the continent in both the United States and Canada, but the Muir family never quite seized its share of the market. After forty years, they were forced to close their mill doors in 1892—the very time the great migration of loggers was heading west.

John Muir & Sons built the first sawmill at Sooke, British Columbia, in 1860.

British Columbia Forest Service.

Captain Edward Stamp.

Sir James Douglas

The American Civil War was a peak for B.C. timber operations, as was the gold rush on the Fraser River. The gold rushes in California and Australia also fueled the sawmills, but only briefly. Market demand was unstable. But the lack of vision was the most damaging of all.

Most British and Canadian businessmen could not gain a foothold—not because they lacked the experience, or the imagination or even the capital—but because they were not properly connected with the powers that be. One exception was Captain Edward Stamp. While picking up spars in the Puget Sound area, he perceived a profit-making situation. Returning to England with his cargo he informed the wealthy Anderson family, of shipping fame and owners of James Thompson & Co., of his findings. As with most things in those days involving business and great distances much time had to pass. In that time Stamp procured ships to carry lumber, found British financial capital and British government subsidizing. Just as the contract was about to be signed by all parties, the British government fell. The successor cancelled the contract. This could have written an early *finis* to another attempt to log British Columbia timber, except that Stamp turned to the Anderson family and Thomas Bilbe of Bilbe & Company. Now, business was business to these two firms. They realized money could be made; the United States was entering a civil war. That meant the American lumber producing states in the East would be out of competition. The gold rush, at that moment, was still going strong on the Fraser River. There were gold and silver strikes being made not only in the American West but also South America and Australia. There were also British colonies throughout the world that needed lumber. The Andersons and Bilbe were willing to back Stamp.

Governor Douglas of British Columbia had long promoted opening the northern territory. He was probably very relieved when Gilbert Malcolm Sproat, a highly respected representative of the Anderson family, approached him with a letter of introduction signed by the Duke of Newcastle. This man was no "American Adventurer." Here was an Englishman. The result was that Douglas gave Sproat 2000 acres for settlement purposes and up to 15,000 acres in timber rights.

It was a coup that could have made American lumbermen gnash their teeth. Those few who knew about the timber deal simply sat back and cleaned their fingernails with forks during the dinner hour. They knew what would happen—what always happened to British Columbia sawmills in those early years.

Having cleared the path, Sproat chose Alberni Canal for the logging settlement, which became known as Anderson's Mill. By 1861 lumber was passing through the mill. This tremendous excitement lasted until . . . 1864. The timber had been cut back away from the mill to a depth of almost eight miles. Sproat recommended a railroad be built to haul out the timber. Possibly because they realized the American Civil War was ending and lumber competition would again come from the Americans, or because of other unknown factors, the British firms refused to put more money into the mill. In the most productive forestry district in British Columbia in the year of 1864 a successful sawmill had to close down because it could not get logs out of the woods.

It was lack of vision that prevented British Columbia's lumber industry from flowering as quickly as the American logging operation. In reverse snobbery, the Americans laughed at the class system that had been transplanted to British North America. Recognizing that the British officials considered them in the same rank as "savages," the Americans didn't especially care. They were after profits in a nineteenth century unregulated market. They were in a hurry; they were rude, ruthless, determined, devil-may-care-as-long-as-there's-a-buck-to-be-made. They were gamblers all, both good and bad, surviving in harsh times and conditions. There were also many more of them than British North Americans for the Americans were polyglot, a restless mass of immigrants and emigrants all seeking a better life—better than the one in the Old Country or in the stony New England states or the war-torn Southern land. So the force driving Americans was different than the one in British North America where most of the people had some connection with Britain . . . or France; for these people the ruling class still remained English. There wasn't an aristocrat in the American bunch—at least an American had better not admit it. What transpired below the Canadian border was strictly survival of the strongest in a commercial street brawl that had no place for gentlemen. The early American capitalists took what they wanted any way they could, for if they didn't somebody else would.

Singer Sewing Company, 1901.

Victoria, capital of British Columbia.

In a less rambunctious atmosphere, Canadian business—the timber industry in particular—grew, sometimes floundered and failed, but other men continued the idea of creating a timber industry. During it all, British Columbia entered Confederation in 1871, and the Canadian Pacific Railway spread its steel tracks across the massive Canadian frontier. The fledgling lumber industry in British Columbia was given a financial boost for the coming railroad needed wood for railway stations, roundhouse, bridges, snowsheds, cross-ties, bunkhouses . . . .

Even so, the B.C. lumbermen found it extremely difficult to compete with the Americans. Despite the railroad, all along the northern bays and inlets, sawmills were closing down while the American sawmills happily tooted steam whistles and rushed logs through buzzing saws. The Americans could ship rough lumber to British Columbia and still underprice the local product. Finished wood products such as carved woodwork, doors, furniture and window frames were exported from California or Oregon or Washington to British Columbia.

With the Fraser River gold rush over, the population dwindled and the economy stagnated. Only the promise of the standing timber could save them.

Into the western United States and Canada the men of the East with money in their pockets were coming for the last stands of timber. For British Columbia the men of the East came from England, Scotland, Quebec and Nova Scotia. For the American Pacific Coast, the men of the East came from the logged-off Lake States and New England. In both cases, these eastern lumbermen not only knew their business, but they had capital, markets and connections. Some even planned to stay.

As for the loggers, they went where the jobs were whether it was Canada or the United States. The loggers drifted back and forth across the border. It didn't matter whether they were Canadian or American, Swede, Finn, Pole, Norwegian, German, French, even an occasional Italian or Greek. All that mattered were their skills in the woods for each man had a specialty.

The jobs for loggers moving west was along a strip that ran from California into Canada. So the loggers continued their westward trek. In the East they had been "shanty-boys." In the Lake States from the 1870s to 1890s they were lumberjacks or just plain "Jack." But on the Coast, they were loggers all, no matter of what national origin.

30

Hard work, long hours.

British Columbia Provincial Archives.

A forest giant, fit for seven men.

3

Skid Road

The loggers heard bragging about the size of the trees along the West Coast, which they quickly dismissed as tall tales. Timber just didn't grow that big. They had to see it to believe it.

Holy Old Ole, if the stories hadn't been true. A man had to lie on the ground to see the tree tops—which wasn't really possible since the giants were as thick as hair on a dog's back. Besides that, the underbrush was a jungle of growth tangled into poisonous plants of Devil's Club and nettles. The brush had to be swamped out before an axe could be swung.

One old-timer when looking over the forested Cascade ribs said, "It's good timber country all right enough, but it's so all-fired rough I wisht Hughie had run His harrows over it afore He was finished a-makin' it." Hughie was the loggers' affectionate term for God.

Logging was going to be a lot different from the Lake States. It didn't snow enough or freeze hard enough to log by sleigh. To cut down a tree so big that the first branch was eighty feet above the forest floor created a problem in moving it. Damn if the trees didn't contain a hogs-head full of pitch. Double damn that the first cut had to be eight feet up which meant using swing boards. Just how were they going to get those giants to the sawmills?

The lumberjack had to re-learn his trade and his legend grew as big as the trees around him. Even his name changed: he became The Logger.

The forest that confronted them, then and now, is narrow with a width from thirty to 150 miles. The strip runs north and south for a thousand miles. The eastern borders are the Cascades and the

Sierra Nevadas. The mountain ranges are scattered with various trees. Inland are the pines—Idaho White, Ponderosa and Sugar. To the west are the California Redwoods and moving north into Oregon and Washington and B.C. is the king known as Douglas fir.

New methods had to be learned, usually whenever a problem arose. The loggers did first what they knew. They attacked the forest from the beach-head along the Columbia River between Washington and Oregon, and the Clearwater in Idaho. Rivers were convenient for driving logs to market. The wild river drives started again. Even in the west the logs were chuted into the water at the peak of spring freshet. If the freshets were not high enough, extra water was released from splash dams. Like weather, water conditions were fickle. High water could cause logs to tumble down the river, break the boom, and continue to the ocean. There was even the possibility of a few or all of the logs sinking before reaching market.

In Idaho "river rats" transported logs from high country to mill on the Clearwater. A six-man crew would follow the log drive in a

The "Dancing Annie," of 1909, a supply boat used on a river drive.

34

long wooden boat called a bateau. This canoe was light, maneuverable and as swift as the logs being driven. From the bateaux, strong men guided the canoe to logs stuck on rocks and sandbars.

Later the bateau was supplemented by the wanigan. This was a floating home for the crew. Measuring about 125 feet in length and containing two bunk houses, fore and aft, it also had a cook house and dining hall in the center. The crew ate meals and slept at night in the bunk houses.

Sometimes river levels would drop during a cold snap, stranding logs. The rearing crews would scramble aboard the wanigan for as long as it took to get those jammed logs off river banks, islands and sandbars. With caulked boots and cat-like agility, they leaped from log to log, using brute strength and leverage to untangle the mess. The shout of "she's hauling" would ring across the river. Men would leap to safety for the warning had been given the jam was breaking up.

The C.L. & B Company river crew of 1906, on the Chippewa River.

35

Standing timber from around the river banks receded and the loggers went after it. The environment wasn't their concern.

The skidroad was invented to bring logs to riverside. A path was cleared in the forest. Felled trees lay at intervals across the path. The limbs were cut off and the trunk was buried half-deep into the ground. In the center of each cross-piece was a rounded notch that served as a guide for the log. Bark was peeled from the bottom of the log so it would slide better. During the haul-out of logs, the grease monkey ran behind the team and ahead of the turn of logs, dabbing the notches with grease. His was a dangerous job and the worst-paid, for if he fell the team continued to pull the logs—over him. There was also the chance of being kicked in the head by the team. Or the bullwhacker would oblige instead if the grease monkey didn't understand profanity.

Skidroad at Bordeaux. This rare photograph was the pattern used for the bron relief seen at the entrance of the Washington State Legislative Building.

British Columbia Forest Service.

In 1894 Canadian loggers pose with peaveys, oxen, and horses.

From the skidroad came the expression which meant city tenderloins—*skidroad*, corrupted into *skidrow*. At one time Henry Yesler had a skidroad for his mill in what became downtown Seattle. The mill eventually shut down, card rooms, stores, saloons and neglect grew up around the skidroad, but the old term remained . . . which is how winos came to be on the *skids*.

The most expensive item to a small-time operator was his skidroad team. A good skidding team was worth $600. Oxen were stronger than horses. Slow, dependable and stupid, oxen plodded over the skidroad. Unlike horses that would quit when tired, the oxen continued pulling until they died. If an ox was killed, the operator hauled the carcass back to camp and fed it to his crew.

A team of oxen was too expensive to waste because a bullwhacker made a mistake. If a bullwhacker "sluiced his team," he seldom lived it down. To kill a team was stupidity beyond belief. Such a man was low enough to oil the hinges on a skunk's stinker.

Driving the team was the bullwhacker who hollered and cussed until the bark of trees smoked. His thunderous shouts and extensive knowledge of profanity was impressive enough to give him top pay of as much as $100 a month plus board. He earned it— he worked sixteen hours a day, six days a week, and he cussed and snorted every minute of it.

Next in rank came the hooktender who made up the turn of logs. He supervised the logs hitched together with chains and dogs. To take care of hangups, he followed the haul-out and cursed almost as well as the bullwhacker. The hooktender (sometimes called the hooker) was head man of the choker crew on a skidder.

37

A logger wasn't a logger unless he knew about choker hooks. The purpose was to find a way of hooking a choker cable to the main line quickly and easily. The hook had to stay fastened when being yarded to the landing and also easily unhooked. An eye-splice was dropped over an open hook on the butt rigging, or a hook on the choker was hung on a ring on the main line. This could be hooked and unhooked easily. Partly closed hooks were experimented with. Each had drawbacks. The present choker is not a hook, but a socket which slides up and down a short wire rope which is the choker. The "hook" is slotted to take the ferrule of the choker which can be stuck into the socket. It is released by turning it at a right angle. Few logs are dropped in yarding with the socket choker hook.

This is a rare photo of rolling a veneer block with team. This was one of the earliest methods employed in the Pacific Northwest. Faster more efficient means were developed.

Jones Photography; Aberdeen, Washington.

Pearl Hazel Rasanen.

Rolling Veneer Block with team.

Horses were used in the yarding area.

Ken Kildall.

38

Elk Creek, Doty, Washington 1910-1912. Yarding poles and logs.

Various choker hooks were invented: Ashdown, Bardon, boxing glove, butterfly, Dennison, jail, latch, Peters, Wirkkala, to name a few.

The handskidder was the hooktender's helper. He carried a maul to drive the dogs into the logs when he made up the turn. A maul was a piece of equipment greatly prized. If he was a good handskidder he carried it into the bunkhouse during wet weather. He might even keep the maul in his bunk when sleeping.

From the skidroad, logs were sluiced down a water flume into a river for the drive to salt water. A Puget Sound or Columbia River sawmill squatted at tidewater and a town would eventually grow behind it. The heart-throb of a lumber town was its mill which was the destination of the logs.

The logs were herded between long boomsticks, chained together and left floating until a tug showed up. The tug hitched a cable to the boom and towed the raft to a mill.

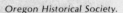

Oregon Historical Society.

The Ostrander sawmill in Oregon.

Oxen were beasts of burden not to be hurried. They set their own pace. For all the goading in the ribs, they refused to be rushed. Logging by oxen on the skidroad was slow and inefficient. John Dolbeer changed that by inventing a new kind of donkey engine. This donkey engine had a single cylinder and a horizontal engine with a drum. In August, 1881, Dolbeer bolted his invention to a sled of timbers, threw a switch and introduced big-time logging. The invention, naturally named after him, had a line pulled by a capstan. The line yarded or led logs along the ground. The oldtime

Loading donkey at McCormick
Logging Co. 1921.

Author's photo.

Turvey Bros. Logging Bucoda,
Washington.

Author's photo.

High-lead logging with a steam
skidder.

40

One of the first models of a single
drum donkey on a skid road.
Clemon's Logging Company, Montesano.

loggers standing around Salmon Creek near Eureka, California during that historic moment had no use for a mechanical marvel. They didn't think it would work. If it did, it wouldn't last.

After the Dolbeer came the Humboldt, Tacoma, Willamette, Seattle, Crackerjack, Duplex and Halfbreed. Whatever the name, the donkey engine crouched and grunted in the yarding area near a railtrack—another mechanical marvel that reached deeper into the woods than the skidroad.

Another marvel for logging was the skidder used for skidding and loading. First invented by Lidgerwood Logging Company in Michigan in 1882, it was improved upon by an employee named Dickinson. Lidgerwood was first used in the northwest in 1904. A skidder was developed from a three-drum pile driver by Horace Butters about 1883. Civilization in the form of machines was invading the woods—it made the more crusty old-timers grumble.

The men who built the first skidroads became, usually, tyee operators. Tyee in Chinook means Chief—anything large and awe-inspiring. Up from the skidroad, the tyee operator knew his job, his men and his equipment.

King tyee of the Columbia River loggers was Simon Benson who invented the Benson raft. He was the first to use a sea-going log raft in 1906. His log rafts were designed for rough ocean water, being cigar-shaped and heavily chained to resist storms. The raft could be as large as fifty-two feet wide and 1,000 feet long containing 120 to 160 tons of chains.

41

A cigar raft being guided by a tugboat on the Columbia River.

As an inventor of sorts, Benson also came up with the unprecedented example of keeping his camps running during the Fourth of July annual drunk. For loggers who had spent months in deep timber the Fourth of July and Christmas drunks were their twice-a-year events of "going down to splash," "hitting the mahogany" or "getting teeth fixed." He hired mostly Scandinavians, preferring those who spoke no English at all. Even so, the immigrants learned enough English to know the Fourth of July was a time to get drunk. Around the middle of June, Benson had barrels of whiskey hauled into his camps. The crew drank themselves sick. Of course, no work was done for two or three days but when they sobered up enough to go back to work, they were told the Fourth of July was past and that they had had their summer drunk. They worked when other camps were shut down. Benson's added bonus was not losing his crew in town to jails, other operators and crimps seeking crews for hellships.

While that may have been considered a dirty trick, Louie Saldern pulled a dirtier one. He ran a "logger's college" on the Lower Columbia. Loggers have to learn the trade somewhere—usually on the job. Saldern made a point of finding greenhorns. He offered to the greenies a logging course that offered board and a little spending money. Eventually, a greenhorn discovered others who were learning the same thing in different camps got paid a regular wage. Somehow, Saldern always found "students" who believed he was offering them a good deal.

#2 Slackline Skyline Machine built by Seattle Iron Works at Peell 1926-1927.

Ken Kildall

Two million ties stacked near Hawkins Creek, British Columbia.

Falling crew and surveyor paused
for a well-earned rest.

4

Axe & Haywire

Inventions speeded logging. Yet the chief tool of the logger remained his axe. Before the advent of the crosscut saws in the 1870s, lumberjacks felled trees even into a headwind with an axe. The scarf on wood was so smooth the mark of a blade was barely discernible. Like the maul to the handskidder, the axe was prized by the faller. If he went to church, which was seldom, the logger sat through the sermon and held his axe. It was enough to make a preacher nervous.

During the winter, most loggers wore beards. Only on special occasions such as a big blow-out did they remove the growth—with an axe. The logger sat on a deacon seat in the bunkhouse and, using a whetstone, brought the axe blade to razor sharpness. Then he would slap soapy water on his face and shave.

Almost as important as the axe was the haywire with which hay was bound for the oxen and horses. The haywire was used for stretching a clothesline across the bunkhouse, for the cook's kitchen utensils, for busted chains and split peavey handles. Haywire bound together the cookstove. Haywire came to mean all that was broken, busted, crazy or unlikeable. A haywire camp was a place with faulty equipment and the worst of everything from bosses to cooking. The opposite to a haywire camp was the "candy side" in which the crew of a high-lead camp had the best equipment. Haywire permanently appeared in the American language.

Single spool yarding engine.

Deep Timber Camp

A man didn't have to stay at a haywire camp. He could leave anytime. The main concerns of a logger were the camp cooking and decent sleeping quarters.

The operators in deep timber had a saying: "There's a crew coming in, one on the job and one moving on."

A logger carried his bindle from camp to camp. If he caught bedbugs it was time to buy a new bindle and move on. There was always one more camp on the line.

A typical day in a logging camp was the same as all the yesterdays and all the tomorrows. At four o'clock in the morning the boss shouted, "daylight in the swamp", or "roll out . . . or roll up." It was enough to grumpily roll off the hard boards or, if one was lucky depending on the number of lice contained therein, a cotton mattress. "Daylight in the swamp" was a poor joke in winter for daylight was at least three hours away.

Beating an old saw was the flunky who, as camp chore boy, called the loggers to breakfast. The flunky filled the wood boxes, swept the bunkhouses, helped the cook and was usually the butt of the loggers' pranks. When he beat a vibrating tempo on the saw, the flunky got even with the so-and-so's.

The crew gathered in the grub house where the cook had spent most of the night making flapjacks out of concrete. Even an axe could be dulled trying to cut into the hidebound flapjacks. The flapjacks were just as heavy in the belly. Loggers cursed it would take all day to digest flapjacks that were little better than Swedish hardtack.

At six the boss yelled again, "all out for the woods," which produced cynical grins since the crew was ten or more miles in deep timber.

Satsop Indians were hired by Schafer Brothers.

After the loggers had sweated and worked with slippery axe handles, chains, blocks, mauls and saws that were slick from constant rain, after dancing on the swing boards for hours, lunch time was announced usually with a shout. Since lunch was eaten in the woods, that meant it was a "nosebag show."

As heavy as the flapjacks had been, the pig iron weight was gone, needing to be replaced by a different kind of pig—hairy pork meat. The beans would be a little hard. The coffee had to be clubbed with an axe handle to make it lay quiet in the cup. Hungry men thought it was delicious no matter how bad it was.

The best thing said about such cooking was that it was filling. Some cooks could make any slice of beef tough black. In logging camps on Sunday the cook served the Grub House Special—"monkey." Monkey was a mixture of burned flour, lard and water; a kind of greasy gravy poured over meat and potatoes. It was served with lard spread on biscuits.

48

The worst camp cook wasn't the one who couldn't or wouldn't cook, but the belly-robber. The cook was in charge of purchasing food. He could make a hefty rake-off working hand in glove with the commissary company. The loggers had a cure for a belly-robber. They'd pull his pants down and set him on a hot stove. He served properly purchased chow after that or left camp entirely.

When slops were finished the crew went back to work. At four o'clock during the winter the northern woods became dark. Once again the boss hollered, "all in," which was how everybody felt. The loggers gathered their equipment and returned to camp. Time enough to wash up at the enamel basins lined up outside the bunkhouses.

By 1905 logging camps had cookhouses that served a hardy and filling fare. If anyone became disorderly the cook's flunky quieted them down with an ax handle.

In personal cleanliness everyone had his own method. The more hardy stripped down to black woolen undershirts and splashed lye soap and water up to their elbows and even sometimes on their faces. Others more daintily swished index fingers into water and dabbed around their lips and eyes. As for a bath—well, that just had to wait until the big blow-out.

At six in the grub house, pork and beans were served again with coffee that could eat out a man's guts. Conversation wasn't allowed during mealtimes. Conversation usually led to an

49

Clang! Clang! The hideous, unwelcome clatter of the getting up bell shatters a dream you were having. Around you issue despairing groans and grunts from your bunkhouse mates. You lie there a moment or two dreading the break from the warm soogans. Then you hit the splintered floor.

You belly up to the giant wood heater which the bull cook has fired up earlier and hurriedly struggle into your black woolen underwear, hickory shirt and tin pants and join the rush for the row of tin basins where you scrub the sleep from half-shut eyes.

"In a short time a flunky comes out and with an iron bar plays a tattoo on the iron triangle known in the woods circles as the prune or gut hammer. You join the thundering herd heading for breakfast in the big cookhouse.

"Inside you are careful to pick out your own seat on one of the long benches surrounding the long tables. If you miscalculate, it could lead to an unpleasant interview with the rightful claimant. Little time is wasted on conversation since this is strictly business. The heavy dishes are loaded with mush, fried bacon, and piles of hot cakes. The coffee is coal black and skookum enough to walk by itself. The camp Brains sit together at one end of a table.

"When you are about half-through this pleasant task, several tardy souls burst in. In every crew there are a few sleepy-heads who have it figured out to the split second just how long it takes to make it and not be late for work.

"The hasers gallop up and down the tables delivering loads of smoking hotcakes from the Paul Bunyan-size camp range. Here is where he learned to be ambidextrous. In an incredibly short time a vast amount of chow vanishes, stoking the boys for an energy-burning day. Filled to the gills, you grab your packed nosebag and a toothpick from the box by the door, going out slower than you came in.

argument then to a fist-fight. Nor was hard liquor allowed in camp.

If somebody talked or caused trouble, the flunky yelled, "shut up!" If the logger didn't quiet down the flunky would hit him with whatever was handy, whether a fry pan or a piece of wood. That was his job.

After the evening meal, the loggers trooped back to bunkhouses. There they thawed and dried out boots, hung wet clothing near the pot-bellied stove, made repairs to clothing, smoked a little Union Leader or chewed a plug, listened to outrageous stories, and usually laid down in the bunks. Around nine the boss roared, "lights out!"

That was the logging camp in 1900. It was slightly worse in the 1880s and had not improved much by 1920 according to Ray Jordan who gave a similar description in his *Skagit Valley Herald* column.

Custom Photo Service.

The donkey engine was a powerhouse, often temperamental and stubborn as a mule.

Logging camp bunkhouse in 1905.
Minnesota Historical Society.

An example of the gradual changes that came to a deep timber camp was told by W.L. Trayling of Vancouver, British Columbia, who worked for the Brooks, Scanlon & O'Brian logging outfit in 1920 when he was seventeen. He told the story of "10 Spot" or "Ten Dollar Joe."

"... The B.S.O. was the first outfit to bring in female waitresses as flunkies into the camp," Mr. Trayling said. "Waitresses is the proper word I suppose but flunkies were flunkies to us. You see, the work force in the camps were a little too transient to suit the operators. Some brain at the head office, I guess, thought women would have a stabilizing effect on the men. . . . The result was the direct opposite of that. Bedlam broke loose among the young 'huskies.'

"... Well, logging camps were no places for females, especially the young ones of a marriageable age.

"The men, on the whole, wanted peace after a hard day's work. They were there to work and make a stake and didn't want to see or hear anything about women. Contrary to popular belief, talking about women in camp was taboo. Loggers in general had a great respect for womanhood in those days and for anyone making a remark about a woman, even a prostitute, got black looks that soon shut him up, never to make that mistake again. This mistake was only made by the young and uninitiated.

"Up to this time you've probably been in your carpet slippers, next step is to pull on your Warren-Greens or Currins, being careful not to put too much strain on the laces. Wet ones break easily and if this happens it means bad luck all day. That's no superstition either. And the pessimists ready their extra rain gear.

"You check your smoking or chewing tobacco, or snoosh supply, whichever is your form of nicotine poisoning, to see if you have enough to last all day, and fill your waterproof match box. About this time the Bull of the Woods bawls, "All out." . . . You ride a crummy or an open skeleton logging car out to the tall and uncut. Usually, you came in bone tired. . . . But every mother's son could roll in at night feeling that he had put in a day as an uninhibited man."

51

"As I mentioned before the average logger wanted peace in camp. We came in from work, took a shower, got into fresh underwear and clean pants, no top shirt, and went to the cookhouse to eat . . . no hanky-panky. Well, to see some of those young bucks primping getting dressed as if they were going to a fashion show just threw the old-timers into a snarling rage. . . . Figured they were making damn fools of themselves, not acting like men a'tall.

". . . You know, among men there are always some handsome young bucks, pleasing to the maiden's eye. So consequently and quite naturally, the girls played favorites at the table. In some mysterious manner most of the choice morsels of food kept landing in front of her favorite which naturally brought growls and snarls from the men being ignored, these being directed at the bum she was favoring, never at the girl.

"One mealtime when a waitress was so pampering a young fellow sitting directly from Joe Sanetti, he said to her 'Don't waste your time with that guy. He only gets $4.00 a day. Come over here. I'm a $10.00 a day man!'

"Hence, we nicknamed him *$10 Joe* which later got down to *10 Spot*. Even though Joe only said this as a joke, it stuck."

Good meals often kept a crew on the job longer than high wages.

Weyerhaeuser Archives.

This log was 24 feet long and contained 7,000 board feet.

Loggers worked from three a.m. until dark. In the North Woods dark could come about four or five p.m. After a stout meal, the loggers could hit the sack. Those not especially tired could swap outrageous stories, or play cards if camp policy permitted. Card playing sometimes led to fights. In the Pacific Coast camps, card playing was usually allowed as long as no money was involved. Of course, this rule could not have been enforced if the loggers hadn't agreed for the old-timers knew a card-cheat was more trouble than he was worth.

The loggers devised their own entertainment. There was at least one or two who could play a fiddle or a mouth organ or even an accordian. Sometimes a toe-tapping tune made the men feel like dancing, especially if they were snowed or rained in. At those times, some loggers would tie grain sacks around their waists indicating they'd be the female dancing partner—a few would even mince accordingly to the bold laughter of on-lookers. If the loggers were lucky, they might have visitors attracted by the music—Indians—so they would have a "squaw-dance." Woodsmen swore the Indian women had greater endurance at the dances than the loggers—the women would still be shuffling when the loggers admitted to having enough.

In the Lake States, the logger games in the shanties were as rough as their work—especially for a newcomer. "Buy My Sheep" was a special game for the tenderfoot. The uninitiated was blindfolded, lifted up and dropped into a pan of water.

There was also "Shuffle the Brogue" which obviously was imported from Canada since *brogue* was not an American term. This was the loggers' version of "Button, Button, Who's Got the

53

Button." Seated on the floor with knees up, the loggers would quickly pass a shoe so that the man in the center couldn't see who had it. Whenever the man who was "it" had his back turned, the possessor of the shoe would swat him with it—as hard as he could. It took a husky man to take many blows from a logger's boot, even without a foot in it.

The other game was "Hot Bottom"—a form of mindless entertainment. Usually it happened to a beginner in the woods. The lumberjack would bend over and the others would swat him a mighty blow across the bottom—often so hard the recipient was laid out flat. Then the man on the receiving end had to guess who struck him. If he was wrong, he had to bend over for another blow. Those wise in the ways of the game would slip a board inside their pants.

The favored entertainment for those melancholy evenings that could creep into bunkhouses on wintry evenings was singing. For a time until replaced by popular tunes in the 1900s, the loggers' songs reflected their prowess. *The Shanty Man's Life* which probably came from New England or eastern Canada is one of the oldest and most widely known lumberman's ballads.

1.
Oh, a shanty-man's life is a wearisome life,
Although some think it void of care,
Swinging an axe from morning till night
In the midst of the forest so drear,
Lying in the shanty bleak and cold
While the cold stormy winter winds blow
And as soon as the daylight doth appear
To the wild woods we must go.

2.
Oh, the cook rises up in the middle of the
     night
Saying, "Hurrah, brave boys, it's day!"
Broken slumbers oft-times are passed
As the cold winter night whiles away
Had we rum, wine, or beer, our spirits for to
     cheer
As the days so lonely do dwine
Or a glass of any shine, while the woods
     alone
For to cheer up our troubled minds

3.
But transported from our lass and our spark-
     ling glass
Those comforts which we here leave behind
Not a friend to us so near as to wipe the
     falling tear
When sorrow fills our troubled mind.

4.
But when spring it does set in, double hard-
     ships then begin
When the waters are piercing cold
And our clothes are dripping wet and fingers
     benumbed
And our pine-poles we can scarcely hold
Betwist rocks, shoals and sands gives
     employment to all hands
and the rapids that we run, Oh, they seem to
     us but fun
For we're void of all slavish fear.

5.
Oh, a shanty lad is the only lad I love,
And I never will deny the same;
My heart doth scorn those conceited farmer
     boys
Who think it a disgraceful name
They may boast about their farms, but my
     shanty boy has charms
So far, surpassing them all,
Until his death it doth us part, he shall enjoy
     my heart
Let his riches be great or small.

Another logging song, *Fine Times in Camp Number Three*, was transported from the eastern United States and Canada and carried to the Lake States, but never gained popularity along the Pacific Coast.

Fine Times in Camp Number Three

1.
Oh, come all you young fellows and I'll sing you
    a song.
It's only two verses and it won't take too long.
It's all about lumberjacks, you plainly see.
REFRAIN
We had fine times in Camp Number Three
2.
Oh, the first of all was our jolly old cook.
He kept regular hours, and he'd call us to chuck,
And then you would hear him in the dead of the
    night—
You would hear him and he'd holler that it's
    almost daylight.
3.
Oh, the butcher he'd cheat on the weight of the
    meat,
And so would the baker on the bread that we'd
    eat.
They would tip up the scales, and they'd lower
    them down,
Say we had good weight when we'd lack half a
    pound.
4.
Oh, the next was our sawyers, and they'd make
    a saw bind.
Their electric light concentrate you could not
    find.
They would grind up their axes, to the bush
    they would go,
And to see them clean up boughs, it was a
    grand show.
5.
Oh, there was a big team they named Paddy
    and Queen,
and it hauled the best loads that you ever had
    seen.
They would pile and they'd load the load ever
    so high—
If the harness stood pat he would load them or
    die.

6.
Oh, there were two big teams—they drove four
    in a row.
As a usual thing he got stuck every load.
And then you would hear him swear loud as
    could be:
"Get up there in the traces, or it's crow bait
    you'll be!"
7.
Oh, we had an old blacksmith, and you all
    know him well.
He would burn all the coal on the side of the
    hill.
He would burn all the coke and likewise the
    charcoal,
And his hooks would not catch in a thing he
    could hold.
8.
Oh, here's to our foreman, and a very fine man,
And he tried to get out all the logs cut by hand.
But he never got rich, and I'll tell you the cause:
'Twas he went much to often to visit the
    squaws.
9.
Oh, we had a young scaler, and you all know
    him well—
He got stuck on himself like a dizzy young
    swell.
He got stuck on himself while he scaled a big
    log.
And he could not tell punk from the end of a
    hog.
10.
So it's now to conclude and not make it too long,
I hope I have said and done nothing that's
    wrong.
For my name it is Watson as you plainly see,
And I drove three big horses for Duncan and
    Dee.

Loggers pose with the woman who
worked as a cook.

6

Fashionable Attire

Loggers wore tin-pants into the woods. Tin-pants originally were heavy, hard-wearing material which loggers covered with water repellent. As the loggers wore tin-pants, the material was further covered with pitch and dirt which made them stiff. When a logger could stand his tin-pants in a corner, it was known he was an experienced logger.

If he didn't wear a good $1.50 Hickory shirt, he had a wool shirt made water repellent by dipping the shirt into a mixture of water and alum. He didn't wring it but hung it up to dry. When the shirt was dry, the logger could wear it in a downpour and keep dry— except around the shoulders where the suspenders soaked in rain.

The tin-pants were staged around the calf to keep the pant legs from being caught up, threatening life or limb. Under the shirt and pants he wore black wool underwear that kept him warm no matter how wet he became. Sometimes he'd wear two shirts at a time. He also wore a double pair of socks in heavy boots. Most loggers slapped a woolen cap or a slouch hunting hat on their heads. A logger's jacket was a woolen, plaid mackinaw that kept out the driving wind and rain.

Most important of the logger's uniform were the boots. Boots were often specially made. A logger's life depended on the fit of the boot and the sharpness of the steel tipped caulks that had to be razor sharp to sink into wood.

In the winter, feet were tortured with chilblains, more so if the boots didn't fit. The cure was to soak feet in hot salt water, rub them with kerosene and stand barefoot for half an hour in the snow. A few loggers sprinkled red pepper into the socks.

Some loggers got around the high price of clothes. There was a faller in Oregon who was built like a grizzly bear and about as friendly. His nickname was Tarzan. He never wore underwear no matter how cold the winters—just his tin pants and shirt. He was so tough he did the work of two men. Fallers worked in pairs but Tarzan worked alone. If the company sent out another faller to help, he snarled at him to leave. He didn't want any "damn partner to try to figure what he was gonna do." His constant "partner" on the other end of the cross-cut saw was a rubber inner tube which he lashed around a tree and fastened to the handles of the saw. By himself he pushed and pulled the misery whip.

Ken Kildall.

Griffith Logging Company, D
Washington.

A logging camp with "modern" bunkhouses.

Steam skidder crew.

Scene in the woods.

7

Man Bites Bear

The logger was a timber beast; hard-muscled, brawny, mean, cussing, dirty and full of fight. He was usually single, always transient and probably the toughest man to come down the pike. He had no use for dudes or men who couldn't handle what came in bottles and corsets, who couldn't fight, who was Joe-college and who was a company man.

Such a man was constantly moving from camp to camp. Invariably somebody had to command the turf. Just about every night there was a fight in camp until one recognized champion was the cock of the walk.

When there weren't any more men to fight, loggers could always do what had been done at Maple Falls when a fight pitted man against bear. Entertainment was in short supply in the deep woods. Loggers found their own rough brand of recreation.

The odds were on the bruin that had clawed out an eye of the last challenger.

This round the challenger was a bull of a man with powerful arms. Waiting, he watched the owner of the bear prod it. The owner had $200 riding on the bear. In fact, most of the loggers had bet the bear would win.

Around the crowd of shouting men the forest was black as the night that pressed down, lighted only by the roaring campfire. From inside the shack the bear growled, slapping at the pole, knocking the owner down. Grumbling, the black bear strolled into the circle of men. Red firelight reflected from the bear's eyes which glowed with hatred for its tormenters.

To get the fight started the challenger slapped the bruin's head sharply, leaping back when the bear growled and flashed sharp, yellow teeth. Its small eyes rolled intently as the logger danced

Straining at the "misery whip," this logger works his way up from underneath the log.

around the bear. Rearing on hind legs, the bear moved in lumbering gait. The logger stopped dancing. He waited until the bear was closer before he struck a resounding blow to the bruin's neck. Staggering back, it dropped to all fours, shook until its loose hide quivered. Suddenly it was up, slashing at the logger and grazing him. The logger rammed like a billy goat into the bruin's belly. Too slow in his retreat, the logger was seized by the bear and held in a crushing hug. It dug claws into the man's back. Its sharp teeth snapped around his head.

All around the spectators yelled, certain the bear would win.

Pressing caulkboots into the bear's legs, the logger hunkered over and squeezed strong hands over the bruin's windpipe. The bear's eyes rolled. Bubbling sounds came from the throat. With a final shake the bear slumped to the ground. A referee counted to six then announced the challenger as the winner.

Bets were paid. There would always be another fight, another challenger.

Another sport entirely the loggers' own was birling, better known as logrolling. Once a year, usually around the Fourth of July, during a series of contests men pitted their techniques against each other. Two men would get on a log that floated in a mill pond or a river. They'd turn it to see who could ride the longest. It wasn't simple. Logbirling has many fancy tricks, turns, and twists. The sudden reverses and stops dump losers into the water. Different logs float high or low and the slickness differs whether the log has been peeled or is still in its natural state. Pine, spruce and hemlock all roll differently. A cedar bolt rides high in the water. A big blue—a large butt log with much taper—has its own problem in balance.

The turn of the century brought in official rules, although unpublished, with judges and prizes. Contests were announced months in advance. Every river had its recognized champion who practiced most of the year spilling lesser opponents into the pond.

Their play was as hard and as deadly as their work.

This log was 120 feet long.

62

Canadian loggers "burl" logs in a rough and tumble contest during the 1910 Cowichan Bay Regatta.

Bucking a huge Douglas fir by hand, late 1920's.

High riggers atop a 250 foot spruce
tree in British Columbia.

8

The Spar

Death was and still is a brother to loggers. It stands silently by a logger's shoulder, waiting patiently for an opportunity. At any time life could be crushed out of a man. When that happened, the loggers of that particular crew passed a hat to pay for the funeral expenses. If the logger was married, the other loggers contributed a day's pay to help the widow.

No matter the job, the logger accepted the risks. If the job didn't kill a man, a time on the town surely would. In the meantime, the cook and flunkies went about camp chores. The swampers went ahead to cut away the brush. There was timber to be cleared.

Titles for loggers changed with the introduction of high-lead logging. The trade-off between life and death grew at an accelerated pace.

Following the swampers the fallers came in to fall trees. They cut above swollen bores where bark was eight to twelve inches thick and the wood was hard with pitch. About eight feet above the ground, notches were ripped into the tree and four-foot springboards were driven in. On the springboards placed on either side of the tree, the fallers balanced as the board swayed up and down. Swinging axes in perfect time, the fallers chopped down the tree.

T-i-m-b-e-r-r! The warning shout sounded through the woods. Loggers sought cover as the giant shuddered. Slowly the Cyclops angled, tearing from the stump. Branches ripped upon contact with other trees. Huge limbs flew to rain upon the slow-moving men. In a soft whoosh the falling fir gained momentum. More branches cracked like rifle shots. In a shattering explosion the tree hit the forest floor and the ground shook. The falling of a tree had its own strange magnificence and violence.

Buckers cut the fallen fir into sections and sawed off unbroken

branches. When the log was finished by the buckers, a chokerman forced a heavy wire noose around the log, wrestled with the cable and attached it to the choker. A chokerman required skill, brute strength and fast legs. As soon as his job was completed, he hastened away and waved at the whistlepunk. The whistlepunk signaled the donkey puncher who waited for the whistle that a log was ready to yard. Throwing in the throttle the donkey puncher set into motion the cable that yanked the log into a free swinging motion crashing into trees, stumps, brush and sometimes a man.

The hooktender, who had inherited the top spot formerly held by the bullwhacker, watched the operation. The hooktender or hooker still watched for hang-ups although he no longer supervised a turn of logs being hitched. If a log became hung-up on a low stump he was expected to move the log by brute force and rank profanity that very often worked. Loggers said all hooktenders were the off-spring of the Devil and Molly Hogan. When words failed, the hooktender threw his hat on the ground and jumped on it in frustration. Sometimes the hooktenders even howled. Some hooktenders went down in loggers' word-of-mouth history; Flying Thompson, Tin-ass Mike and Jimmy the Bear.

Weyerhaeuser Archives.

Steam donkey engine loaded on railcar for moving.

highclimber looks over the untryside from atop a spar.

A load of logs being brought in on a high-lead system.

When the hang-up was cleared, the hooktender dropped his hand in a signal and jumped clear. The whistlepunk pulled his chain. The donkey puncher threw in the throttle. The donkey engine grunted and groaned and carried on in jerky protest. The drums spun and the slack of the steel cable snapped with enough force to tear a man apart. The log, about forty feet long and six feet thick, wheeled across the yarding area and crushed to splinters anything in its path.

From "ground lead," logging went to "high-lead." Instead of pulling logs across level ground, the donkey engine yanked them into the air to swing them into the yard. High-lead logging doubled the output in the woods. It also doubled the accident rate.

When a logger was hurt on the job, he had to wait until the end of the shift before he was carried back to camp. If Death took its opportunity, the steamers which left the deep timber camps often carried on its flat car under a sheet of canvas the busted-up body of a logger.

An integral part of high-lead logging was the spar—a tall, limbed tree cut off at the top so a block could be hung 150 feet or more from the ground with the cable from the donkey reeved through the block.

Making a spar was the job of the high-rigger, also called the high climber. His was the glamorous job of the woods with the best pay. He was considered an artist with his life rope knotted in steel rings, long-spiked climbing spurs strapped to boots and legs. He climbed a tree with sheer muscle power, lopped off branches and topped the green crown that plunged to the forest floor throwing up dust and debris.

Author's photo.

This was called a Unit. It was used for yarding and loading simultaneously.

68

Using his spurs, the high climber climbed up the tree which was often as tall as an eight-storey building, curved the rope up about ten feet for the next hitch on the spar tree pole. A half hour climb adequately covered the remaining 180 feet or so from the first seventy feet of base. A cut was made. The crown was sixty feet high above the cut. He leaned back on his life rope made of manila line with wire cord—strong enough for a man's weight but easily cut by the sharp axe if the topped spar should splinter and spread with the rip. In that position he slashed a deep notch opposite the falling direction of the crown. Lowering the axe on a line fastened from his belt, he pulled up the saw for the amputation of the top.

Quietly the top plunged to the ground until it made a thunderous crash. While the crown tumbled, the spar swayed, vibrated, quivered and shuddered. The high climber rode it out until the bucking stopped.

Sometimes the high climber climbed on the severed top that was often four feet in diameter to look over the country. He had earned his right to show off on the spar by standing on his head or doing a little jig. Other times instead of doing a jig, the high climber threw off his cap, slackened his belt and raced the cap to the ground. Using his life line in slackened and tightened drops, the high climber swung to the ground in a dozen hitches. Going down was quick, but not easy. It took skill and required letting the rope drop ten feet below the spurs. He would swing out and fall, sinking spurs into the wood, and would drop the rope again for the next hitch.

A spar tree.

British Columbia Provincial Archives.

A high-rigger poses with his gear.

This complicated piece of equipment looked good on paper but was a flop in performance. It was never used again.

Sometimes a top was blown off. The high climber used the same techniques for climbing except this time he girdled—shelved—the tree about six inches deep around the diameter of the tree. Into the rut he placed about seventy-five sticks of dynamite in bundles of five and set a six-foot long fuse. If he hadn't rigged a light block on a line for quick descent he had to come down by hitches. If he had done a good job when he lopped off branches he did not get hung up and was down the spar in less than six minutes. Time enough to be clear of the dynamite blast that could sever the top as clean as a saw cut, hardly doing damage to the spar six feet down. That was a dynamiting high climber who knew his job.

High-lead logging was high-ball. Men worked faster. Operators offered a "yarding bonus"—the boss set a footage mark, purposely high, for a crew. If the crew yarded more than the mark, every man received a dollar or more added to his wages for that day. Some hooktenders became exuberant trying to make a name by consistently reaching the "yarding bonus." Such hooktenders aroused the ire of loggers. Accidents could happen to hooktenders sometimes more easily if they forgot they were loggers, too.

High-lead logging was thought to be the last word in logging. That is, until somebody thought of using two spar trees. The skyline system or "flying machine" was born. A taut cable ran between two spars. The cable was about 150 feet above the ground and on the cable was a device called the bicycle. With this system logs zipped to the landing of railroad cars and were loaded by McLean loading booms or other tackle. Logs swung around curves, up and down mountains, over canyons without once touching the ground. The speed was breathtaking.

Bob Barr at the Bridal Veil Lumber Company in Oregon is credited with rigging the first skyline in the Northwest. The year was 1899. Logs could be moved out of the woods even faster.

Hayrack booms were used for loading flatcars and trucks.

In front, surrounded by logs is a "one-man saw." It took three men to handle.

A donkey engine—1917.

The one-million dollar trestle.

72

9

Million Dollar Trestle

As the timber receded further into the hills, the operators built stupendous trestles across yawning canyons. Some trestles contained enough logs to keep a sawmill running for a month.

Trains, owned and maintained by the timber companies which had put in rail-tracks, hustled and bustled with twenty, fifty, even 100 flat cars piled high with logs. The trains zoomed around hairpin mountain turns, over dizzy high trestles, all rushing to take the big sticks to the waiting log pond.

No cost was spared for the "logging show." Weikswood (Washington) had an impressive one-million dollar log trestle for the haul-out. In the early 1900's a million dollars still had substantial buying power.

One old timer who was around during the building of the timber company railroads said he and a friend were working on a crew building a trestle. His friend accidentally tumbled over the edge. The falling man disappeared among the tree tops. It was a long way down to the bottom of the canyon. All that could be heard was the breaking of branches. He was a goner for sure. The crew wasn't allowed to quit work for rescue operations of a dead man. An hour later the man climbed up the side of the canyon and went back to work. The tree branches had broken his fall. Except for a few bruises, he was feeling just fine.

The logging locomotives were called locies. In the early years the toy-like locies ran on wooden tracks. Most were made by local ironworks, sometimes even by the company. The Ant is credited with being the first locie in Washington. This six-ton saddle tank was a wonder.

These little locies that sometimes went as high as the 120-ton Mallets operated by Booth-Kelly Company were the prime

A snag stops production.

Satsop River bridge.

Locomotive.

Japanese laborers.

Portable bunkhouses on flatcars.

An 1883 Climax locomotive.

movers of logs in the Pacific Northwest during the years of 1890 to 1930.

When the woods shrilled with the music of train whistles, there were over 460 railroads, over 6,700 miles of tracks and about 1,230 locomotives.

Almost every major logging operation was a railroad show. Some were even famous for their railroads such as the Kerry Line which ran from the Nehalem Valley to the Columbia River in northwest Oregon.

Many, such as Schaffer Brothers with extensive land holdings in Grays Harbor and Mason counties, Washington, had spur lines. But all things must end. Because some outfits had as many as twenty-one locies a substantial log yield was required to meet the expenses. The trees disappeared quickly around the railtracks. That, combined with economic depressions, closed down hundreds of deep timber camps. The locies were scrapped—sometimes even put on public display by major logging companies. Only the tracks remained, until the rails, too, were ripped out. In the early 1960s the Schafer Brothers tore out the spur line that ran into the upper Satsop. Even the track bed is disappearing under a tangle of briars, brush and sturdy new conifers.

Author's photo.

There's more than one way to climb a hill. The grade at Weikswood was so steep the train engine couldn't climb it. After building a $1,000,000 trestle, the operators weren't about to be stopped by a "slight" grade. After much head scratching a solution was found. Placed at the top of the grade was a donkey engine with a cable running along poles much like telegraph lines. In this way the train could be pulled to the top and carefully lowered again.

Many companies had stores which offered everything from food to clothing.

Sundays

Sunday was the loggers' day of rest. Unfortunately they were so far back in deep timber, there was no Saturday night brawl to repent. On Sunday a logger could shave if he had a mind to. Or read if he knew how. Some patched clothing. Most played cards such as poker and used tobacco for gambling stakes.

In every camp there was a short-stake man—a man who never stayed long in any camp. He was constantly on the move seeking that paradise camp that had no lice, excellent food, no muzzle-loading in the bunks, and high pay. A short-stake man might work a few days or as long as a month. His paycheck was his stake and it was never quite enough. He would sit hunkered over in his bunk, squinting at a dog-eared, greasy-thumbed timebook that listed his debts to the company store and his coming pay. He figured and re-figured, ciphered and stewed with a pencil chewed down to a blunt lead point. No matter how he studied on it, he could never win although in the back of his mind there would be another camp up the line much better than the present one and the thought that one day he would have enough to set aside to relax. He scratched at his whiskers, grunted and considered the items bought at the company stores. The company store charged twice the price in a regular store. It also didn't have much competition being twenty miles back in the brush—the snoose had cost a frogskin ($1.00). Union Leader tobacco was thirty cents. Overalls two dollars. Gloves, shirt at a dollar and a half. Lordy, Lordy, there was no way for a man to get ahead on forty-five cents an hour. He would have to work a week to for the company just pay off debts. By the end of that time he knew he would have certainly added to the debt. He refigured again, hoping he had misfigured and that the next time it would be to his advantage. The short-stake man was not one for conversation, but he was easily made content on payday.

Sunday was a day for boiling up—washing clothes. This was done with a squeegee—a logger's homemade washing machine. This was made by nailing a tin can to the end of a strong stick, open side of the can downward to make a vacuum.

However, only sissies washed a shirt when it could still be bent.

The real problem was little critters that made a point of moving in on a man. Body lice were known as seam squirrels or pants rabbits. The varmits could be removed by "reading your shirt." Those caught and which were too tough to squash could be exterminated by being dropped on a piece of hot tin with a candle underneath. The best way all around was to leave the shirt on an ant hill for a few days. The ants never missed a louse. For the lazy man there was the "walk the bugs to death." Simply turn the shirt inside out and make the bugs walk to the front.

Sunday was also a day to talk about the last and the coming blow-out which came in intervals of six months. The stories loggers told—those that could be printed—were outrageous. They talked about the whingety-whong-whang-whoo bird which slept with its head in a very peculiar place and had to be impolite to get it out again in the morning. There was the bird that ate red pepper and flew backwards to cool off. And the side hill gouger which had two long legs on the downhill side and two short legs on the uphill

In a Canadian logging camp, it's "boiling up" day—Sunday. A time to boil the "seam squirrels" out of flannel shirts and underwear—a time to be shaved—a time to read and maybe relax.

British Columbia Forest Service.

side. It couldn't get off a hill. If it turned around it would fall over. As a result it kept going round and round the same hill. The side hill gouger laid square eggs that also couldn't get off the hill. It was coarse as a buffalo rug on the downhill side and scaly as an alligator's hide on the uphill side, caused by rubbing against brush.

For all the tall tales told an immediate hush would fall over the loggers when the French Canadian spoke. Their distinct accent added flavor to the story. Seldom able to read and write, the French Canadians had a vivid imagination and lively hand gestures. Their sense of humor and touch of irony left the loggers rolling with laughter.

Somehow stories told with a French Canadian accent seemed funnier but lost impact in translation. One concerned a lumberjack who was blithely dipping his oars through a Minnesota lake. Spying a moose, the lumberjack lassoed the moose. Terrified, the moose struck for the forest, towing the lumberjack and canoe over rough ground. As he hung on for dear life, the lumberjack's whiskers whipped the trees. The friction made sparks fly, starting a raging forest fire. The spread of the fire was stopped only when rangers shot through the rope, releasing the bawling moose.

Greenhorns were told to watch out for the fearsome creature, the "agropelter." The agropelter was mightily upset having his woods invaded by loggers. From Maine to Oregon, the agropelter had a deadly stroke. Anyone who had encountered the agropelter never lived to tell what the creature looked like, except it was known the creature lived in hollow trees. Anyone who passed by the agropelter's shelter received such a blow on the noggin' that he was thought to have been killed by a falling limb.

Another fearsome creature was the "Indians' Devil" which ripped its victims to pieces with its huge claws and sucked all blood from the body. Just as dusk would be enlarging shadows in the forest, loggers would whisper to a greenhorn that they could hear the Indians' Devil a'moaning in the woods. Sure as it rained, the creature was a'thirst'n for human blood, having a special liking for greenhorn blood, since it was still so innocent and sweet and all.

The "High Behind" had a high behind and a taste for human flesh. It ran backwards over its victim so it wouldn't leave any tracks, and snatched off the victim's head, which was its favorite eat'n.

Some cynics needed more tangible evidence before believing. So loggers would point to porcupine tracks which can be found all over the woods. Those tracks belonged to a fearsome creature, the loggers warned, sure as there is a God in Israel. If the tracks were disturbed a terrible calamity would happen to the loggers. This story was usually told a swamper brand new in any woods job. The swamper was quietly told to lay out the roads so as not to

Deserted bunk houses.

A modern bunkhouse on a flatbed railroad car serves as an office.

disturb the tracks—which he did. When the foreman saw the winding road, his bellowing at the swamper could probably be heard all over the woods.

The Hugag was certainly a cousin to the side hill gouger, residing only in northern Minnesota and western Wisconsin. It was big as a moose with jointless legs. It had a long upper lip. Its head and neck were hairless. At night it rested by leaning against a tree. Hating humans it would remain perfectly still until the intruder passed by, then the Hugag would fall on him.

When the loggers got tired of stories they poked fun at each other by describing a thin man as one who had to stand ten minutes in the sunshine before making a shadow. They would get out their Copenhagen tobacco and chew. No man was a logger unless he chewed and the brand was always Copenhagen. With the decline of logging camps and that breed of logger, Copenhagen now has to advertise for customers.

Some men couldn't handle being in deep timber too long. The old saw to that was: If you don't like it, draw your pay. Nobody says you've got to stay. It's a free country.

When that happened, the logger went to the timekeeper and said, "make'r out." He was quitting. Or he might say, "got'r made" which meant he had his stake made. Others said, "mix me a walk." No matter how they said it, they were leaving. Among those who couldn't stay long in one place were the "camp inspectors," so called because the tramp logger was constantly on the move. A bet was made between two Oregon loggers to see who could work the most camps in thirty days. The one worked thirty camps. He lost because the other logger worked thirty-one.

Hard hats came into use in the 1930's.

Employees of Buchannon Mill, Olympia, Washington, 1930.

Logs await mill work in the Cass Lake, Minnesota, boom. The year is 1920.

11

Log Rustlers

Much like the cattle country trail herds, logs were driven to market—by river to the sawmill. Also like the trail herds there was a danger of rustlers. Contraband logs sold cheaper than legally marketed logs. Those sawmills dealing in rustled logs bought low and sold high. They were said to be timber short and money mad.

At the sawmill logs were herded between long boomsticks which were chained together until a tug came to tow the log raft to another location. There was a raft of rafts to choose from—ocean-going rafts; Baker, Benson, Davis, Gibson, Robertson, Wheeler-styled rafts. Thousands of rafts. One or two logs could be stolen, or a section uncoupled. Some pirates with guts would take an entire raft.

During high tides or rising water, logs were washed out of booms like strays in a cattle roundup. Beachcombers grabbed the strays legally from the beaches. Only when beachcombers or log pirates grew greedy was there trouble. Pirates watched for an unguarded log tow, uncoupled the last section, timing it so that the raft would drift with the tide, then round up the logs for the sale.

Brands were used on logs to cut down piracy. Each owner had an identification shape, legally registered, that was hammered into the butt end. The pattern could be letters or numbers or a combination of the two. It would also be a character brand. One Tacoma firm used a bear's foot. A Montesano logging concern had a six-pointed Jewish star. The only trouble with branding was that the log butt end could be sawed off and rebranded.

By 1923 in Grays Harbor County, Washington, logs totalling $100,000 a year had been stolen. Log patrols of loggers and sawmill men were organized. The idea spread to Port Gardner, Everett, Bellingham and other sawmill towns.

The heyday of the log pirate was from 1917 to 1928. In 1928 the State Log Patrol put the kiwash to the whole business. W.E. Craw, former Everett police captain, was put in charge. He obtained eight fast tugboats provisioned with rifles and revolvers. The crew was comprised of deputy sheriffs who had to be navigator, detective, sea lawyer and seaman.

Craw used operators who posed as boom men and log-pond men. Men in those jobs were usually the bribery targets of pirates. His actions uncovered strange facts. The log pirates were not random operators, but were organized.

The trail led through an owner, general manager, superintendent and head boom man of a well-established Seattle sawmill concern. In this operation entire booms, or entire sections of booms, were stolen and cut at the Seattle mill. The trial eventually climbed the ladder to the officials of one Puget Sound county.

What finally ended log piracy was the Great Depression when logs became worthless.

The tugboat "Ada Barrett" tows a log raft.

A barge for the M & L Company eases a log raft on the Columbia River near Steila, Washington on July 14, 1916.

Men inspect the chains of a log raft on the Columbia River.

A long drink on a hot day.

12

Booze, Brawls, Bawds

Most lumber camps paid in gold. Camps like Pope and Talbot had no pay day. Their men were paid in cash, every night if they wanted, at the company's big general stores. Or they could "leave it lay" until they were ready to quit or were fired. That was their system of pay for three generations.

Some camps paid with a check. If a man was in a hurry, the check could be cashed at the camp company store for a ten percent discount. However, banks recognized camp paychecks. So did saloons.

Whether they grew sick of the woods or went to town with other loggers for their blow-outs, there were places to spend their hard earned money.

Skidroad had a carnival atmosphere of penny arcades, shooting gallerys, a mission with free soup and a sermon, a tattoo parlor—which might have a display of a basket of China tea, a bottle of American ink, soap, and cigarette advertising cards. To the knowledgeable that meant a Chinese lottery. Skidroad had barber schools where students gave free shaves and haircuts to bums. There were also barber shops with lady barbers. Mixed with the noise were demonstrations of medicine shows or a painless dentist using a stooge. After 1906 there were union halls and International Workers of the World (I.W.W.) halls. At the top of the logger's list, rather than soul-saving or political ideologies, were whiskey and women.

Skidroad was Trent Avenue in Spokane, Burnside Street in Portland, Yesler Way in Seattle, Pacific Avenue in Tacoma, Hume Street in Aberdeen, Gastown in Vancouver B.C. and Market Street in Everett with its infamous Bucket of Blood Saloon.

Loggers migrating from Maine to the Lake States to the Pacific Northwest brought with them names out of their past—Hotels Michigan, Saginaw Rooms and Bangor Houses. Restaurants were called "The Loggers Waldorf" or "The Cookhouse." Saloons were named "High-lead" or "The Pines."

The most infamous of all the skidroads was Portland's lusty old North End which was almost anything north of Burnside Street.

Whenever a logger needed to describe something that was larger than life, he said "bigger than Erickson's." Erickson's bar ran 684 lineal feet. Founded in the early 1880's by August Erickson, a Russian Finn, the bar grew until it occupied most of a city block. It had five entrances (one entrance on each street plus an extra one obviously for the bouncer), a concert stage, a mezzanine with private booths for beverages, food and love-making. Of the latter, the ladies were not on Erickson's payroll.

Art decorated the saloon walls. The most famous painting was of an auction sale of Roman captives. Many a patron was found to be crying into his beer while drunkenly contemplating the implications of the painting. Also a place of culture, the saloon had a $5,000 grand pipe organ.

Free lunch was served with paid drinks. Such standard items included half of a roast ox. The smorgasbord included lots of sausages, buckets of pickled herring, and a variety of cold cuts. Along with Swedish hardtack was soft bread for sandwiches which were put together by the patron. The price which included the feast? Beer was five cents. Hard liquor was two for a quarter.

Erickson's, like any good saloon, had a crew of bouncers. Requirements for the job was to be bigger and tougher than the loggers and sailors frequenting the establishment. Jumbo Reilly was a crew all by himself. He weighed 300 pounds. Although he couldn't fight well, his bulk was menacing enough.

A story was told of a confrontation between the slow-moving giant, Jumbo, and a sawed-off runt called Halfpint Halverson. Halfpint, when in his cups, would be more full of fight than usual. He became so obnoxious in Erickson's that Jumbo picked him up and bounced him into the street. Halfpint dusted himself off and re-entered Erickson's by another door. Jumbo threw Halfpint into the street. Like a bouncing ball, Halfpint bounded in through another door, and right out again. Halfpint was not to be deterred. He merely went to the next door, out again into the street. Jumbo anticipated Halfpint would appear at the fifth and final entrance. He stationed his mountain of flesh before that door. Whereupon Halfpint came eyeball to navel with Jumbo. Halfpint looked up slowly and roared, "Holy Old Mackinaw, are you the bouncer in every damn saloon in this town?"

Erikson's Saloon located at Third and Burnside in Portland, Oregon,was a "must-see" for every logger in the Pacific Northwest.

Portland's North End hosted many an exciting boxing match.

89

Part of Erickson's legend was the refusal to be closed down by man or nature. In 1894, Portland, which faces the Columbia River and is dissected by the Willamette River, was inundated by a flood. All business ceased. Gus Erickson merely chartered the biggest houseboat he could find, stocked it with supplies and the famous free lunch, moored it in the middle of Burnside Street and threw the doors open to business. Before long rowboats were tied to the houseboat. Word spread. Anything that floated, including an occasional logger riding a bobbing fir log, was paddled to Erickson's. At Erickson's nobody cared about the flood, except that it gave them an excuse not to leave.

As long as the bouncers were as big as Jumbo, the gender didn't matter. Mary Cook was the bouncer in her establishment, The Ivy Green—sometimes called the Poison Ivy Green. She was tall, raw-boned and weighed 285 pounds. Sometimes she would bodily pick up a misbehaving logger and hurl him outside. Most of the time, she wanted to give him something to remember so he wouldn't cause trouble in her saloon again. Her favorite method was to lift a logger in her arms, carry him outside and skid him along the planked sidewalk. As he picked the splinters from his backside, the logger swore never again would he arouse the ire of Mary Cook. She wasn't a hostile woman. Business was business; she didn't want her place busted up by a rowdy.

Oregon Historical Society.

The Hotel Zue Rheinpfaltz, Portland, Oregon.

Mary liked to stand near the barroom entrance and nod to the customers when they entered. She smoked long black cigars. Whenever a customer held out a finger to her, she would obligingly and skillfully blow smoke rings around it. Three in a row for good luck, a smile and a wink.

Liverpool Liz was short on looks. She made up for that in finery. Her gowns were the best. She never appeared in public without her famous gold and diamond necklace reputed to weigh four pounds.

Liverpool Liz tolerated no rolling of a drunk in her place. Whenever a logger with pay ripe for spending came into her place and only four customers lounged at the bar, he would yell the drinks were on him. It was hospitable and with a few customers he would get by cheap. As the words came out of the logger's mouth, the bartender pressed a hidden button to alert the girls upstairs. Down the stairs came about twenty girls, giggling and calling for free drinks the logger was buying. A round of drinks at Liverpool Liz's could cost five dollars.

Ralph Reed.

Paddlewheeler.
Ralph Reed.

Paddlewheeler on the Columbia River.

Loggers called Nancy Bogg's bordello a floating hellhole where anything could be bought. She ran one of the earlier houses of prostitution in Portland when it was just a fur and sawdust town in the 1880's. At that time Portland was two towns separated by the Willamette and each town had its own law officers. Whenever the law tried to close her down in one town, she would weigh anchor to her two-storied houseboat and drift to the other shore. Her houseboat was eighty by forty feet with the lower part a saloon and dance hall; the upper floor was living and working quarters for the girls.

Nancy Boggs moved her houseboat according to the arrival of steamers, the river current and the dictate of public outrage. Customers had an unfortunate habit of falling over the side of her houseboat and drowning. That, combined with the depravity of her girls, raised a hue and cry. Law officials of the two towns got together and raided her joint at the same time. Fighting back, she hosed the raiders with hot water while her girls jumped overboard. In mid-stream Nancy was on the twisting horns of a river current dilemma. She made a hasty escape in a rowboat. In that precarious craft she appealed to a river boat captain who was watching the entertaining episode from his ship. He went after her run-away scow and saved it for her. He was amply rewarded with a complete run of the houseboat and rescued girls. Anchored at mid-stream, Nancy thumbed her nose at the law.

The Pioneer Building, Seattle, Washington.

The Fountain Saloon, Portland, Oregon.

When it came to class none could hold a candle to the Paris House which catered to loggers. Located on Davis Street between third and fourth, the Paris House was in the heart of Portland's North End. It was a rambling, block-long building of which only the second and third floor was used by the Paris House. One hundred girls labored there—white girls were on the second floor and all other shades were on the third.

In Seattle it was not genteel to call prostitutes by their trade classification. Whenever a soiled dove was sent to jail, she listed her profession as seamstress. The tenderloin had more seamstresses than any other part of town—which must have caused endless embarrassment for those ladies who were actually seamstresses and performed no other service than sewing.

Usually fallen women were easy to recognize for it was obvious what was really for sale. Only when police were responding to public cries to clean up the tenderloins did the soiled doves go underground. At those times the women surreptitiously hung out signs of the type for which "big-foot Matt" (Mattie Arnold) was infamous. Her signs indicated "real estate for sale" or "fashionable dressmaking." She made the mistake of bragging of triumphing over the law because of the signs. Some things just weren't permitted. One of them was mocking the police. The Seatte police arrested her and fined her $25, likely for felonious language.

Author.

Bull Durham was a "man's tobacco."

Among the most famous of the Seattle notorious ladies was Lou Graham. She was an intelligent, enterprising businesswoman who introduced a "class" house to the area.

In a time when men liked their women quite round, she stood five feet two inches and was three feet thick. Like her Portland competitors she had a taste for plumed hats, flashy jewelry and smart clothes.

No ordinary brothel interested Lou who shrewdly held a meeting with the Seattle (male) Establishment. Like a railroad tycoon she used facts and figures (the dollar kind) and pointed out what Seattle needed was a Class-A brothel. Not another tidewater crib joint abounding on the tenderloin. Portland was famous for its decadent tastes at any price, but there was no establishment north of San Francisco that catered to the top hat and black tie set. Her girls, selected from around the world would not only be exceptionally beautiful but highly intelligent. Her girls would be able to discuss politics, economics, the world and human conditions all the time supporting the weary head of a businessman on a voluptuous bosom.

An 1889 fire destroyed downtown Seattle.

Washington State Historical Society.

Not only would she provide a traditional soothing service, Lou, and others in the trade, including the allied fields of liquor and gambling, would add economically to the city coffers. All told, that sinful segment of Seattle's society would provide eighty-seven percent of the taxes, fines and license fees to the city's General Fund.

In addition, she imposed a fair trade standard. In her establishment the price would be the same for everyone regardless of wealth. Included in the price was assured anonymity, safety of personal possessions in the house safe, and if a customer needed a physician's care as a result of visiting her house, she'd pay the bill. Lou would charge $2 a customer, the same price for all. If the customer chose to stay overnight, the price became $5. Along the way she mentioned accommodations were always available to representatives of the city government at no cost any time of the day or night.

What Lou wanted in return was backing from the Establishment. No police had better raid her house. During the public outcries to clean up crime and end prostitution, the police could target in on the tenderloin.

Lou's business acumen and the Establishment's greed led to the opening of Lou Graham's place on the southwest corner of Third Avenue South and Washington Street. In 1888 the lot cost her $3,000 and is now prime downtown real estate.

Eighteen months later Lou's place went up in smoke during the Seattle fire of 1889. She came back with gusto having become wealthy during the brothel's operation. She built a three-story brick building even more elegant—or more pretentious—than the previous one. At the same time she bought $25,000 worth of fire damaged lots, merely as an investment and a belief in Seattle's future. With the proceeds from her business she also invested profitably in stocks and bonds.

Lou believed in tasteful advertising that became an art form in Seattle. On Sunday afternoons, she and her girls in their best finery would be displayed in a carriage while "taking the air" on main streets. Regally, Lou waved grandly to onlookers. More demurely, she nodded to customers, careful never to compromise them.

In 1890 Harry White became mayor and was told by the proper citizens to crack down on the scandalous goings-on in the tenderloin. That meant a round-up of prostitutes.

As fate would have it, who was to be arrested at the first shot? Lou Graham, arrested by a policeman who claimed he didn't even know who she was. It hit the newspapers like a bombshell.

Read all about it! Notorious Madam arrested! The proprietress of the most notorious house of ill-repute. . .

A posh bar—1890.

Lou was not abandoned. The Seattle (male) Establishment selected two prominent men to represent her in court—J.T. Ronald who had completed a term as prosecuting attorney for King County and would become a Superior Court judge in King County, and Samuel Piles. Piles had been Assistant District Attorney under Ronald and would become a United States Senator from the State of Washington.

With good reason Lou was not particularly worried. She put on fancy clothes and jewels, gathered together her most beautiful girls and went to court.

The trial attracted so many people that the building housing the courtroom swayed with the mob, threatening to fall down. Ronald bellowed his way through a defense as each witness claimed not to know anything, not to have seen anything or not even to know Lou Graham. The jury was told to deliberate the case. In three minutes they returned with a verdict of Not Proven.

Needless to say, Lou was never arrested again.

Who brought the railroads? Who was on a first-name basis with men of influence? Who financed politicians and a Seattle jeweler? Who brought in the headquarters for the Mosquito Fleet? Who bequeathed a quarter of a million dollars to the Common Schools in King County? Who was credited and blamed for everything, probably including the Seattle fire? Blame it on Lou, boys.

Lou profited greatly from the wages of sin but the fair trade standard was harsh competition for the girls in the streets and cribs. They had to earn less and work harder to gain customers. That resulted in the fallen women becoming more lethal than loving. Understanding how much of their professional money was being funneled into the city treasury and that the police turned a blind eye to prostitutes (all the more since Lou's trial), they went after customers with both hands.

Or trap doors. The cribs often were located over tideflats. Many a customer after being served knockout drops in a drink found himself in a muddy bed under a cribhouse the following morning. Some never woke up at all. Bodies littering the shoreline disturbed local administrators.

A city ordinance was passed forbidding trap doors on the Skid Road.

Another problem arose with the prostitutes who had found easier ways of getting money than going to bed. The accident rate of being hit on the head by flower pots went up as quickly as the crime rate. After being disposed helpless into the gutter, the victim, upon awakening, would also find his wallet gone.

A city ordinance was passed prohibiting flower pots in windows above the first floor.

Every sawdust town had a tenderloin, a district of red lights or "the line" that separated the naughty from the proper. The saloons were not palatial. A bar was often planks thrown across empty barrels. The floor was double thick to withstand assaults of caulkboots. Sawdust was thrown on the floors. Trap doors were standard equipment in waterfront saloons for the shanghaiing of potential sailors.

There were saloons and there were saloons.

Custom Photo Service.

The Summit Bar was the first tavern and social hall in McCleary. Here the logging camp and mill workers "hit the mahogany."

Such as "Our House." Seattle was not a loggers' town although it had its beginnings in sawdust. Being a crossroads for shipping to and from the Orient and Alaska, it was more a sailors' town. Which might explain partly why "Our House," which was the most illustrious saloon in Seattle, didn't allow caulkboots.

Most saloons, to keep the logger trade, merely replaced the floor as part of business expense. In Seattle loggers who wore caulkboots went to other saloons such as Billy the Mug's which always had a fistfight going.

Seattle saloons differed from the old-time Western saloons that were a place mainly to drink and gamble and maybe get into a fight. Seattle saloons had vaudeville. In fact, vaudeville was born in Seattle. Box house saloons originated in Alaska and the sourdoughs brought back the idea to Seattle. The box house saloon contained a stage for entertainment, thus, vaudeville.

From the Seattle box houses which were combination saloon, theater and dance house came the vaudeville kings of the Twenties: John Considine and Alexander Pantages.

"Our House" was ready for boxhouse entertainment since it had been a former theater. Green tile dressed the bar. Huge pillars flanked gigantic mirrors. In overhead bordering panels were intricate carvings. The outside walls were decorated with false barrel-heads, each with the slogan "Only Straight Whiskies for Our House Patrons. We Could Buy Them Cheaper But We Wouldn't. We Would Have Bought Them Better But Couldn't." Twenty-five games on the second floor gambling hall continued as long as the customers could.

Yet for its larger size, Seattle couldn't compare with the lumber town of Aberdeen. Located in Chehalis County, later to be called Grays Harbor County, Aberdeen had the famous Humboldt Saloon, Hume Street, and most of the sawmills and the logging camps. For action, a logger went to Aberdeen to make his stake or meet his death.

Until 1905 when the Aberdeen fire leveled the Humboldt Saloon, no logger in Chehalis County could say he hadn't been in the Humboldt. The Humboldt was an institution. It was also a tourist attraction and strongly recommended to all male visitors. No woman, good or bad, was allowed in the Humboldt. Nor was any fancy man tin-horn gambler.

The Humboldt stood on the corner of Heron and F Streets. Big Fred Hewett was the owner. To Big Fred, the only real man was a logger. All others were lesser breeds. An ex-logger from Maine, he watched over fellow loggers with a paternal eye. Loggers who came to town for a blow-out could leave their money in Big Fred's safe and know they would get it later. Big Fred had simple banking rules. He placed a logger's money in an envelope, wrote the logger's name and amount of cash on the outside and gave it back to the logger when the logger was sober. A logger couldn't get his money if he was drunk. Not even to buy drinks at the Humboldt. Big Fred cashed about $600,000 worth of checks. How much the safe held during the celebrations only Big Fred knew.

After a blow-out if a logger had spent all his money and had to work again at another camp, the Humboldt supplied him with a bottle of "a little of the hair of the dog that bit you." Big Fred never worried about the expense of supplying free liquor or even about lending money to down and out loggers. Asked one time if he had lost much money that way, Big Fred responded, "maybe five dollars."

Fred Hewitt's famous Humboldt saloon also served as a museum.

The Humboldt was also a museum for it had showcases of curious articles from around the world brought into the Humboldt by sailors. Big Fred's collection included pieces of minerals from mining regions across the world including two pieces of diamond ore with sparklers. From the South Seas and the Philippine Islands were weapons, fishing gear and tribal costumes. From Australian bushmen to the American Indian had been collected weapons, clothing and medicine. There were bugs, snakes, birds; moose and elk heads and antlers; guns of every size, shape and period,

"Bottoms-up!"

The Port Townsend hotel catered to "swamp angels."

many with histories; a knife collection; old coins; photographs of logging days; rare stamps; photographs of murderers and their victims; freaks of nature preserved in formaldehyde; a piece of stump cut by a stone axe. Curios of every kind and conversation.

Such a place brought in many visitors. One time a visiting Easterner leaned across the Humboldt maghogany and ordered a Manhattan. Silence filled the saloon. Stunned patrons peered to look at the stranger. Some wondered what the hell a Manhattan was. Hewett never raised an eyebrow. He poured a slug of gin equally with rum, a dash of brandy, bitters and aquavit into a beer mug, topped it with beer, stirred the brew with an oversize forefinger and slid it down the polished bar.

"Drink 'er down," he ordered.

Big Fred never allowed fights in the Humboldt. Because of his size and reputation, his rule was obeyed.

Other saloons were less fortunate. Once a fight started between loggers, no-one interfered. A fight was for blood with broken bottles, hardened fists and sharp caulkboots to the face or gut. Whatever came to hand was used. It didn't matter how a man fought, just as long as he won.

During its annual Loggers Fourth of July Celebration, alternately hosted by the neighboring cities of Aberdeen and Hoquiam, a fight could easily be had. Aberdeen had twenty-eight saloons at the time. Since much of the city revenue came from this source, the police didn't interfere much, so the saloon-owners maintained their own brand of law enforcement, usually with a mallet. Over a majority of the saloons was a "rooming house". In Aberdeen the cribs and parlor houses extended from F Street on the Wishkah River to the salmonberry swamps to the west. While women were not allowed in the Humboldt, no such ruling applied at the four huge dance halls: The Palm, Monterey, Two-Step and The Empire. Most of the girls were in their teens. Where they came from nobody asked or cared. They could leave whenever they wanted. If they did, they could be found in another lumber town doing the same "play for pay" work.

Money talks, but in Aberdeen an out-of-work logger could get by on credit. The Butte Cafe in Aberdeen devised a system other eating establishments soon followed. For cash a meal ticket could be had for $4.50. But if on credit, the cost was $5. When on credit the logger signed an authorization for a payroll deduction against his future job. A logger could at least eat as long as he was out of a job, even if it was for several months. But the Butte never lost a dime for eventually every man-catcher seeking employees for a lumber operation ate at the Butte. The man-catchers were told to get the man a job, which eliminated bums who wouldn't work.

Even the rooming house Madams had a similar system, so an out-

100

of-work logger always had a bed . . . and company. By the time the logger went back to work he was deep in debt.

The saloon-owners made themselves good buddies by giving a down-and-out logger, needing a drink worse than a preacher needed a sinner to save, a "free drink." Any whiskey, beer, wine or whatever left in the bottom of a glass was never thrown out. Instead, it was dumped into a common bottle beneath the bar. The bottle had a funnel in its neck and was often placed next to the sink. Instead of being dumped in the sink, the liquor went into the "dregs" bottle. As a public relations gesture the barkeeps gave the dregs to the broke logger.

Being a saloon owner was not without its peculiar problems. When it came to music there was no pleasing a logger. Especially more than one logger. Especially drunk loggers. All wanted a favorite tune played at the same time. The saloon owners learned to keep their musicians behind the protection of a chicken wire cage. A sign hung on the wire enclosure proclaimed: " The man who pays the dollar, names the tune."

Sometimes the music was downright terrible. When a fight started, a howl went up whenever a logger lifted his opponent overhead and was ready to smash him against a wall: "Don't waste him; kill the fiddler with him!"

The fights were a way to get rid of pent-up frustration from the months in deep timber. For hours, days, weeks, months, all loggers had seen were other loggers. There was nothing better than a good fight, a bath and massage at a Finnish sauna and a sweet-smelling woman to relieve all that.

Some logging companies had a train run on Sundays from a camp nearest to town. Company men would gather up the drunk loggers and pour them back aboard the train. So blessed, the company train would return to camp so the crews would be full the coming Monday. It was cheaper and less trouble to bring back a drunk good worker than hire a new man. After a roaring weekend in town, the loggers would be described as "so stiff you could rack them up like cordwood on the Sunday night train."

But for the out-of-work logger, with the Butte feeding them, the Madams sleeping them and the barkeeps oiling them, Aberdeen was logger heaven.

A graceful windjammer awaits a load of timber at the port of Aberdeen, Washington.

13

Shanghai

On occasion a logger never got beyond the first drink. Especially if it was a Mickey Finn.

Loggers earned more money than sailors. The gold fields lured sailors to jump ship. Besides, on land a man could pull the pin any time. At sea there was no escape from a Hellship except in death.

A shortage of sailors on ships ready to leave on an outbound tide created a business called Shanghaiing. In the trade it was known as crimping. Whatever the name, the meaning was the same. When ships had a quota of men needed, word was sent out to the crimps who immediately went to work securing victims.

Portland was a well-known shanghai port thanks to "Bunco" Kelly. Most of the saloons crimped or provided for a crimper with a Mickey Finn. There was also another way. While a logger eyed the soiled doves, he was suddenly plunged through a trap door to a waiting boat. The saloons usually hung backsides over the edge of waterfronts. In the boat the logger was bound and gagged and taken to a ship. Among the crimpers there was no honor for the men they sold or to whom they sold.

One time Kelly was faced with a shortage to fill his quota. Not about to let money slip through his fingers, he wrapped and tied a cigar store Indian in a tarpaulin. Kelly packed it aboard and explained to the captain that the man was stiff with liquor; once he had sobered up he'd be fit for the job.

A bunch of loggers whooped it up during one of their hit-the-mahogany events. The party moved from the saloon to the "wine cellar." The shenanigans grew so rough they broke into a basement next door. What they didn't know was that this "wine cellar" belonged to an undertaking parlor. The barrels lining the walls weren't full of liquor but of formaldehyde. The loggers

103

thought they had died and gone to heaven. They quickly consumed the gas. The loggers did indeed die but their arrival in heaven was questionable.

Kelly heard about the bodies lying around and saw a way to fill his quota. He hustled the corpses aboard a ship short a crew and charged an extra two dollars a man with the declaration he had "got these fellers stiff on me own money. . . "

All ports were hangouts for "crimps."It was an easy way to make money: as much as fifty dollars a body. Almost as famous as Bunco Kelly were the crimps of Port Townsend: Limey Dirk with Limey Dirk's Sailors' Boardinghouse. Another trap lay in wait at the Pacific Hotel.

Yet of all the crimps none would be as infamous as the so-called mass murderer of Aberdeen.

Ralph Reed.

Many waterfront logging towns were accessible by boat.

(opposite) Waterfront scenes like these were familiar in all lumber ports.

Author's photo.

Arthur Boose and Stewart Holbrook, of the I.W.W., pose with the Industrial Worker newspaper.

14

The I.W.W.

The Industrial Workers of the World (I.W.W.), better known as the Wobblies, made their bow in 1905. The term Wobbly was credited to a Vancouver, British Columbia, Chinese waiter who said, "I likee I Wobbly Wobbly."

Pre-dating the I.W.W. was the Shingleweavers Union, started in 1901. The shingleweavers fought hard for a union wage scale which was painfully achieved in 1904. While the loggers were fighters—and lovers—it was among the more militant shingleweavers working in mills that the labor force became organized in Washington State.

The shingleweavers were made of sawyers, filers and packers who worked as a crew.

The packers were so skilled in their trade that when they stacked the cedar shingles into overlapping bundles, they appeared to be weaving. Thus, shingleweavers.

A sawyer was recognized by the missing thumbs and fingers on his hands. He sat on an upright machine and faced two flashing, hungry blades which, with machine mentality, lacked compassion. To his left was the bolter-saw measuring about fifty inches in diameter. Feeding a cedar log into the array of belts and saws was a man who pushed the log along by using his knees and hands. A little carelessness on his part and he could easily fall, pulled to certain death. Once the cedar log was sawed into bolts that would fit the carriage, the work continued on an assembly line basis. The carriage ripped about sixty slices. The saw to the left of the sawyer sliced the blocks coming from the bolter while the sawyer cleared it with his left hand and passed the slices to his right hand. With his right hand he trimmed and shaped the shingle on the trimmer saw before passing the finished shingle down a chute to the packer.

During the deafening whine and buzz of saws, cedar dust flew drifting into nose, throat and lungs, blinding the eyes. Meantime, the bosses roared for the sawyers to work faster and faster as the sawyer put out as much as 30,000 shingles in a ten-hour shift.

For each shingle existed the possibility of a mistake that tore into flesh and bone. Eventually a sawyer would make a mistake. Blood would splatter as he lost a finger, part of his hand or his entire hand. Sometimes an arm slid down the chute.

In 1910 shingleweavers through organized labor had fought for and achieved top wages of $4.50 a day.

In contrast the lumber mill workers earned $2.25 a day.

As below the border, the signs of discontentment among the workers started with the specialized millworkers who were often married, a settled part of the community, and were looking beyond their own immediate needs to those of their children. The first strike in British Columbia was at Hastings Mill. It produced no victory for the strikers.

Everett lumber mill yard—1902.

Weyerhaeuser.

Manager Andrew Onderdonk of Hastings Mill had been appointed by a syndicate of American businessmen. He was to carry out their contract with the Canadian government to build the railway from Port Moody to Savona's Ferry through the Fraser Canyon. When the railway work was completed in 1886, a dozen or more applied for work at Hastings Mill. The men were hired at the current daily wage of $1.25. A dispute arose and the men called a strike, walking off the job. Refusing to submit to their demands or listen to interested citizens who tried to persuade Onderdonk to re-think the situation, the manager announced he would hire Chinese and Indians.

As bad as the mills were, the logging camps in the late nineteenth and early twentieth centuries were worse. Since government aid and regulation was lacking, private groups such as the Young Men's Christian Association, and even the Salvation Army, tried to provide social services and medical attention to the loggers. Anglican clergyman Reverend John Antle who had worked among loggers in Oregon lumber camps made a survey of conditions in lower British Columbia during 1904. That report resulted in the Columbia Coast Mission.

While the attitude of most owners of lumber camps was narrowly paternal, they did favor any idea that was a stabilizing influence on the loggers. A. Fitzpatrick, a Toronto clergyman, organized Frontier College—which was not as popular with the veteran loggers as it was with the owners—and sent college students to work in the western mining, logging and construction camps. After work, the young men were given lessons in reading, writing and arithmetic. The more crusty loggers called them college punks as they turned to the I.W.W.

The I.W.W. attracted many personalities—not just the radical. Joining were those who felt they had waited long enough for changes in working conditions. Such men had to be as strong in their convictions for to be a Wobbly was to be a target, to be without work because of Wobbly association. Sometimes it meant death.

Shake bolts are kept to be made into shingles.

The hand that will rule the world—one big ur

15

The Aberdeen Wobblies

Strength lay in numbers. The Wobblies recognized this so they were constantly active in recruiting members. The best way to recruit members was to pick a corner in town well traveled by loggers and millworkers. Up on the soapbox the Wobbly orator would rise and harangue the gathering crowd. Under the Free Speech amendment of the United States Constitution they were within their civil rights to speak out, even blast the government. Sometimes the truth in their accusations hit dangerously close to home.

The Wobblies were not only considered extreme, but downright dangerous, for they were said to advocate radicalism, agitation, violence and sabotage even though their platform was better working conditions and pay. Viewed with hindsight, their demands were not unreasonable.

For that time and place, the demands for the dignity of the working man were certainly dangerous. The blasts smacked of the "red menace" happening in Russia and threatening the rest of the world.

To each extreme there is a counter-acting extreme: those who fear the loss of the status quo. In this case, such soap-box oratory frightened the businessmen and city officials who had nightmares of the working class running amuck, burning down cities, raping and plundering. The reaction was hastily enacted ordinances to discourage such gathering and speech-making.

The ordinances only served for the Wobblies to cry foul and demand their right to free speech.

The Wobblies waged a devious warfare of nerves in every town.

Each time a Wobbly speaker spoke out from his soapbox, the local police simply gathered him up and carted the culprit off to jail. No sooner had the Wobbly speaker been carried away, than another Wobbly would scramble atop the "poor man's speaking platform" and carry on the narrative. Then that person would be arrested, and the next, and the next until the jails were overflowing with "free-speech Wobblies." When the Wobblies were released, stories soon spread about the barbarous treatment received behind bars—unreasonable harassment, mindless beatings, jails so crowded people were forced to stand for hours, men and women prisoners not separated . . .

Industrial Worker, 1910.

The Constitution Guarantees Freedom of Speech. RATS!

Water Cure for Workers   Turkey for Pimps

It is the nature of Americans and Canadians to root for the underdog. The Wobblies were clearly the underdog. The more the Wobblies were arrested, the more they were denounced by newspapers and politicians, the more Average Joe Citizen went to hear what all the hoopla was about. Frankly, the speeches tended to be boring, almost fanatical on the same few subjects. What really brought the crowds was to witness the inevitable confrontation between the accepted and the unaccepted. Perhaps if the Wobblies had been left alone by government, people wouldn't have paid much attention to their speeches.

At any rate, local governments were receiving a bruising from the rumors and were also being hit hard in the pocketbook. While jail fare is never much, the cities were obligated to feed the Wobbly prisoners. Twenty to several hundred prisoners was playing havoc with their budgets. Surely, there had to be another way to deal with the Wobblies.

112

Meanwhile, the Wobblies decided to take their cause into the bastion of lumbermen—to the locale that had the greatest concentration of sawmills and logging camps: Aberdeen, Washington, in July, 1911. They also chose their location quite well for their "free speech" movement. The selected corner was near the hiring hall—"man hunters" or "employment sharks" as the Wobblies called them—which was incidentally near the saloon of anti-Wobbly city councilman, John O'Hara. The Wobblies had a bone to pick with O'Hara. The councilman had loudly denounced the Wobblies, not only in his saloon, but at council meetings. O'Hara had even secured a ban against street speeches in downtown Aberdeen, making exceptions for the Salvation Army and other similar groups.

William A. Thorn was an organizer for the Industrial Workers of the World. Despite what has been said about Wobblies, they did try to work within the system. Only when they were outlawed, did they resort to outlaw tactics. Thorn, joined with fellow supporters, approached O'Hara in the City Hall lobby. They asked that the ban be repealed. Obviously not a coward, even though out-numbered, O'Hara promptly knocked Thorn off his feet with a well-calculated single blow.

That meant war. Immediately local Wobblies wired their national headquarters and newspapers. They called upon their reserves to gather forces in Aberdeen.

Sheet music cover of "The International"

I.W.W. logo.

113

On November 21, Thorn stood on his soapbox at the intersection of H and Heron Streets. He blasted everyone from politicians to mill owners to businessmen to "weak-kneed" officials of other unions. Then he gave his opinion of the Aberdeen police who had been tolerant up to that point. The police carried Thorn off to the hoosegow.

The Wobbly plan went into effect. James M. Train continued the speech. He was summarily arrested. One by one fellow Wobblies climbed up on the soapbox. One by one they were arrested.

The next day the Wobblies were still getting up on the soapbox. When W.I. "Windy" Fisher—whose nickname was well chosen—spoke, he was still talking an hour later without police interference. Recognizing that the police had decided to ignore them, he motioned for his listeners to follow—right into City Hall where the city council happened to be meeting. When Fisher began his speech this time, he was arrested.

Outside, firemen turned hoses on the gathering crowd of Wobblies and curious spectators. The Wobblies were elated, continuing to demonstrate for a half-hour. This barbaric use of fire hoses, they concluded, would create an outflowing of sympathy for their cause.

However, many Aberdeen citizens were concerned about this "radical element" causing a disturbance on city streets. Rumors flew that thousands of Wobblies were coming from all over the country to take over Aberdeen.

The next day Mayor James W. Parks and civic leaders met at the Elks Hall. Approximately 500 other concerned citizens attended. Many joined the voluntary police which would patrol the Aberdeen streets, railroad station, docks and roads. Any Wobbly coming into town would be booted right out.

They also planned to disrupt the I.W.W. rally to be held at the Empire Theater that night. The first thing they did was cut off electricity to the Theater. A citizen police force surrounded the rally site. Armed with axe handles, a vigilante posse swept along the street, arresting anyone who appeared suspicious. The Wobbly leaders plus forty men, including the guilty and the innocent, were taken to jail.

At East Heron Street, the vigilantes broke into the I.W.W. headquarters. Papers, records and other items such as furniture were confiscated.

The next question was: What was to be done with the Wobblies?

About midnight the Wobblies were taken out of their jail cells. In later years and other towns this would have meant a hanging. All the Aberdeen vigilantes wanted was to have the radicals gone. Two men to a prisoner, they escorted the Wobblies out of town. On the east side, outside Aberdeen, the Wobblies waited in the glare of car headlights as bread was passed among them—food for the road, so to speak.

A typical I.W.W. meeting—1915.

One of the local leaders warned the Wobblies, "God bless you if you remain away, but God help you if you ever return!"

While the Aberdeen vigilantes were certain they had put the fear of God into the Wobblies who were walking away from town, the Wobblies were men with a mission.

The set-back was only temporary in their opinion. For the moment they were discouraged, soaked to the skin from both the fire hoses and the chilly November rain, but they weren't done Gathering other Wobblies found wandering in the brush, this hardy band stayed in the neighboring town of Montesano. Here they spun their plots, wrote their handouts, and raised funds. Occasionally, they sent scouting parties into Aberdeen. A few were caught, arrested, beaten and shown the city limits again.

A new Aberdeen ordinance was passed against street speaking of any kind and that included everyone.

By January, things had settled down somewhat. Slipping into Hoquiam, which was beside Aberdeen, Wobblies were aided by believers. Going before the Aberdeen City Council—which was a very gutsy thing to do—Wobbly leaders protested the public speaking ban.

Announcing only peaceful intent, several non-violent Wobblies attempted to open up another headquarters on January 8. A police raid ended this when Thorn and nine others were arrested at the hall. Thorn and his companions were beaten and tossed across the city limits line. The Wobblies returned the same day.

On January 10, 1912 fifteen men tried to reopen a free speech demonstration at Heron and G Streets. The citizen police were alerted by a fire alarm. The free-speech orators were arrested. Possibly high on adrenlin, the prisoners had a jolly good time in the city jail that night, laughing and joking despite the grim possibilities of being taken out and hanged.

Enough was enough, the city officials decided. They had done everything they could to discourage the Wobblies. Business had been hurt. The city was suffering from loss of prestige in their handling of the whole matter. They decided to negotiate.

Conveniently, Mayor Parks found the Wobbly leaders in the city jail. The negotiations started. After two days both sides reached agreements in which the hated ordinance was withdrawn. The new one permitted public speaking in most of downtown Aberdeen as long as there was no interference with traffic and commerce. Some Wobblies could stay, but specific I.W.W. agitators had to leave town. This, too, was agreed on. The I.W.W. was compensated for properties destroyed in the January 8th raid.

Now that the Wobblies could speak anywhere on the Aberdeen streets, they lost interest, looking toward other towns where free speech was being denied and, in particular, to the lumber camps.

In other towns, they would be treated far less politely—even killed.

FELLOW WORKERS: *Solidarity, 1917.*

Remember!

WE ARE IN HERE FOR YOU; YOU ARE OUT THERE FOR US

Jones Photography; Aberdeen, Washington.

A headrig.

Jones Photography; Aberdeen, Washington.

A shingleweaver's occupation was known, without explanation, because of his missing fingers.

I.W.W. members pose in front of office.

16

The Everett Massacre

Wobbly or regular union man, the northern woods became the scene of a revolution. Millworkers and union organizers were hanged or shot, sometimes both. People were imprisoned. There were bloody victims like those in Everett.

In 1916 Everett was primarily a milltown which faced westward toward Puget Sound, a town awhirl with the raspy growl of saws, a pall of bluish smoke, whistles that announced the start and close of a work day. A mill town.

On May 1, 1916 stewards of each mill made presentations, as per instructions from the union strike committee, to each millowner. Each millowner in turn refused to be intimidated by the proposed strike. When the stewards left the mill offices, the sawmill workers left their machines. The saws stopped grinding, smoke faded over the mills and the whistles became silent.

The long strike began.

Tempers pro and con rose.

On Hewitt street was a soap box where orators in the past had spouted beliefs on everything from religion to free love. During the strike, Citizens' Deputies ended all free speech on Hewitt Street.

Rumors spread that the Wobblies would burn Everett to the ground. There was talk of sabotage and arson. Neither happened. The only definite truth was the Great War in Europe which created a demand for lumber in coffins and ammunition boxes. Cedar shakes were again popular. The mills had to be reopened for patriotic reasons. For profitable reasons.

On October 31, 1916 the strike was slowly grinding down when forty Wobblies, all in their early twenties, were stopped by Citizens' Deputies.

What did the lads want in Everett when they weren't local boys, the deputies asked.

To give a speech on Hewitt Street, one said, since such a ban was a violation of the federal constitution.

The Wobblies later said McRae and his deputies had been drinking.

Sheriff McRae said the Wobbly leader had a smart mouth.

Whatever had been said, the conclusion was clear: Like Hell they'd give a speech on Hewitt.

The forty young men were forced into automobiles and driven to the outskirts of town. The remote spot was called Beverly Park. One Wobbly later said that their "pants were taken down." In the thin drizzle of rain the cars had been lined up so that the headlights played over the scene of two hundred men on either side of a gauntlet. Each of the two hundred deputies and businessmen carried tree saplings, axe handles, clubs and rifles. Between howling and cursing men, the Wobblies were beaten with Devil's Club and forced to run under a rain of blows while kicked in the gut until they reached a cattleguard at the end of the gauntlet. Their screams were heard by neighboring farm families.

The beaten Wobblies had to walk twenty-five miles from the Park to Seattle. The next day Wobbly leaders and union representatives went to Beverly Park to check out the story of the Wobblies, many of whom were hospitalized. Although it had rained all night, blood still stained the plants, the churned ground, and the road back to Seattle.

The incident laid the groundwork for the Everett Massacre.

General view of the site of the Everett Massacre.

On November 5, 1916, no one worked. Instead the Everett townspeople stood on the hills overlooking the waterfront. Word had come from a stoolie in Seattle that a boatload of Wobblies were coming to burn Everett to the ground as a result of the Beverly Park incident. The National Guard was pressed into service to protect the town. Sheriff McRae and his deputies were at the dock. What was to be learned almost fifty years later was that the "tip" was false.

The day was clear with a sharp chill. The azure blue sky blended with the slate-blue of the open water dotted by forest covered islands and a wind kicked across the Sound. Puttering over the water was the *Verona*, a small ship which regularly ferried between Everett and Seattle. On board were the usual passengers and over two hundred young men alleged to be Wobblies. Many were likely I.W.W. who had gone to speak on behalf of the strikers and protest the ban on freedom of speech. Many were idealistic college students practicing Constitutional rights theory taught in classrooms. Others were North Dakota harvesters wintering in Seattle who had decided to go along for the boat ride and see what all the fuss was about. The actual number of men on the *Verona* was never known, although history buffs place the figure at 250. So many who had crowded aboard in Seattle did not have the money to pay and were allowed to ride with no accurate record being tallied. Another hundred men went to the *Calista*, same destination.

County Sheriff Donald McRae— 1912.

Awaiting the *Verona* which was due to arrive at 1:40 p.m. was Sheriff McRae and 200 armed citizen deputies. As the passenger ship was being secured to a piling the sheriff demanded to know which man was the leader.

"We're all leaders," came back an answer.

"You can't land here," Sheriff McRae announced.

It was reported later somebody answered back, "The Hell we can't."

Who fired the first shot would never be known. Only one thing was certain—the deputies were armed. A search of the *Verona* later in the day produced no weapons. A rifle volley exploded from shore. On land those in the front ranks were shot in the back by their own men. Pro-Wobbly Everett citizens who had been lining the shore shouting a welcome to the *Verona* passengers screamed during the shooting crescendo. Sheriff McRae was shot three times in the leg, possibly by Citizens Deputies. Aboard the *Verona* men shouted and ducked bullets. Four of the alleged Wobblies were killed, twenty wounded, and unknown numbers missing when, during the rush to the other side of the ship, the *Verona* shifted. Living and dead were dumped over the side. The ship, being ground into reverse, broke free leaving those in the water. Shot from the mast was a young Milwaukee resident who

Tom Tracy, the one I.W.W. member tried for the murder of Deputy Jefferson Beard.

had been waving to people on shore. He was identified as possibly Hugo Gerlot. Also dead were Harry Pierce and Gus Johnson of Seattle and Felix Barran, hometown unknown.

Dead among the Citizens Deputies was Snohomish County Deputy Sheriff Jefferson Beard and Charles O. Curtis, Everett sales manager and member of the Citizens Deputies. The question would become, since the men had been shot in the back, did the Wobblies on the boat shoot them or the deputies?

The *Verona* limped back to Seattle with its terrorized and wounded passengers. In Seattle the police waited to arrest seventy-four Wobblies on the *Verona* for murder. A search of the ship produced no weapons, except for the customary I.W.W. weapon: cayenne pepper.

Newspapers of the day demanded harsh treatment for the Wobblies who had "murdered" the Everett citizens. Seattle Mayor Hiram Gill was called to task as to why he didn't prevent the Wobblies from leaving Seattle.

He answered,"We can't stop people from traveling on boats if they want to go. In the final analysis it will be found that these cowards in Everett, who, without right or justification, shot into the crowd on the boat, were murderers, not the I.W.W.s."

His remark was booed down.

The case went to trial against the Wobblies. I.W.W. member Tom Tracy and seventy-three other Wobblies were charged with first degree murder. Famous attorney of the "downtrodden," George Vanderveer became their legal counsel. Thundering and producing evidence most preferred to ignore, he succeeded, only after a bitter court battle, to have the seventy-three indictments dismissed. The trial was the greatest labor trial of its kind on the Pacific Coast. Vanderveer had researched the events surrounding the docking of the *Verona* so thoroughly he secured the first major legal victory for the I.W.W. He also committed professional suicide. His career came to a dead end. Vanderveer wasn't a man to accept defeat easily. He was heard from again when he defended various members of the Seattle underworld during the prohibition years of 1916 to 1933.

The popular verdict that resulted from the labor trial prompted thousands of men to join various unions.

However, no charges were brought against Sheriff Donald McRae or any of the Everett citizen deputies. Not even for the murder of the four Wobblies.

The VERONA, 1916.

I.W.W. members' funeral.

Laws, State of Washington
Session Laws, 1919
Chapter 174
(S.S. B236.)

Prevention of Criminal Syndicalism

An act relating to crimes, providing penalties for the dissemination of doctrines inimical to public tranquility and orderly government, and repealing Chapter 3 of the laws of 1919.

Be it enacted by the Legislature of the State of Washington:

Section 1. Whoever shall

(1) Advocate, advise, teach or justify crime, sedition, violence, intimidation or injury as a means or way of effecting or resisting any industrial, economic, social or political change, or

(2) Print, publish, edit, issue or knowingly sell, circulate, distribute or display any book, pamphlet, paper, handbill, document, or written or printed matter of any form, advocating, advising, teaching or justifying crime, sedition, violence, intimidation or injury as a means or way of effecting or resisting any industrial, economic, social or political change, or

(3) Organize or help to organize, give aid to, be a member of or voluntarily assemble with any group of persons formed to advocate, advise or teach crime, sedition, violence, intimidation or injury as a means or way of effecting or resisting any industrial, economic, social, or political change,

Shall be guilty of felony.

Section 2. Any owner, lessee, agent, occupant or person in control of any property who shall knowingly permit the use thereof by any person or persons engaged in doing any of the acts or things made unlawful by the preceding Section, shall be guilty of gross misdemeanor.

Section 3. Chapter 3 of the Laws of 1919, hereby repealed. This act shall not be construed to repeal or amend any other penal statue.

Section 4. This act is necessary for the immediate preservation of the public peace, health and safety and shall take effect immediately.

Passed the Senate March 3, 1919.
Passed the House March 11, 1919.
Approved by the Governor March 19, 1919.

17

Criminal Syndicalism

To break the unions and I.W.W., self-interest lobbying groups met in the Washington State capitol of Olympia during a legislative session to urge the passage of the "Criminal Syndicalism" law. Governor Ernest Lister vetoed it but after his death, the next State Legislature passed it.

The law was so vague it could be used to apply to any type of publication and assembly. It clearly drew battlelines. Either one was a Wobbly or one was not. One was pro-union or one was not. One was for the working man or one was not. There was no middle ground.

Criminal Syndicalism was a law that rubbed salt on old wounds. The great strikes of 1917 when workers were beaten and jailed by the thousands were bitter memories to the timber beast, sawdust eater and sawdust baron alike.

The Great War added to the Wobblies' unpopularity for the I.W.W. openly denounced the war with the declaration there were greater battles on the home-front than in far-off Europe. The Wobblies were considered to be in the vanguard of world revolution—such as the one in Czarist Russia.

In 1917 the I.W.W. and the craft unions joined forces and asked the lumber operators for an eight-hour day at three dollars a day for the mills; or an eight-or nine-hour day at $3.50 for the lumber camps. The operators refused.

The lumber operators suffered the "Wobbly horrors." To protect their interests, they formed the Lumberman's Protective Association which could fine any man five hundred dollars a day for working less than ten hours per shift. The operators warned they'd strike with an iron fist if they caught any man "packing the rigging" around their camps and mills.

In July the men left their jobs in almost every mill and camp. The strike of 1917 was on. It lasted six weeks, longer than the men could afford to be off work. The craft unions authorized their return to the job although the demands were still unmet. Among those who returned to work were card-carrying Wobblies, but they urged "conscientious withdrawal of efficiency." In other words, a slowdown. Work eight hours and quit. If you were fired, the new crew would still work eight hours and quit. There had to be a limit to how many men could be fired before the operator lost money.

Thus it went. Slowdown. Fired. Another crew. Another slowdown.

The workers' resistance affected the war effort. Spruce was needed by the airplane industry. Colonel Disque was dispatched by the War Department to straighten out labor matters. After frantic collective bargaining sessions, two organizations were formed which were none too popular with anybody: The Loyal Legion of Loggers and Lumbermen, and the Spruce Production Divisions. Colonel Disque felt that union demands had to be met if lumber was to be cut. He ordered the operators to change work shifts to eight hours, pay time-and-a-half for overtime, and furnish bunkhouses with clean linen. The spruce was logged.

1917 was a year of world war, Russian revolt, international unrest and in the Pacific Northwest a time of strikes in camps and mills. Union halls were raided, torn apart, rebuilt, and re-opened in time for the next raid. Thousands of workers were deported for violation of the Espionage Law. Dozens of Wobblies were mobbed, tarred and feathered. Others were taken away in the night and hanged from railway bridges.

THE REASON

Industrial Worker.

Industrial Worker.

If a man "packed a card," he was a union man. Sometimes he also carried an I.W.W. card and wore the Wobbly button proudly on his lapel. Labor cards and buttons could get a man a free ride on a train (railroad workers were organizing and fighting just as hard as lumber workers), a place to sleep and even job opportunity. It also meant a quick death on a short rope. Such "rigging" could even change the tone of a barroom argument when men gathered in "blind pigs."

Dirty Shirt: "I see by that there button you're one of those clowns from Red Hall."

Wobbly: "Yeah, and I know you. You're a Goddamn stinking Company man."

Dirty Shirt: "I ain't never told on nobody."

Wobbly: "You're a Scissorbill who finks to the Big Push and that's the gospel. You were told last week to hoosher it, but you won't cooperate. This is an organized camp. You don't like it, you can pack your balloon."

Dirty Shirt: "I ain't packin' nothin'. Just because I don't go along with this crap is no reason I should be told to pull my time. I don't want no trouble from you or the Tyee Push. I mind my own business."

"You either join us or leave. Look, Dirty Shirt, the company ain't gonna do you no favors. All you'll get is Pie in the Sky when a widowmaker falls on you. What are you going to leave for your family? We're not trying to start a bolshevik revolution. All we want are decent wages and living." The Wobbly spat Scandihoolvian dynamite into sawdust sweepings. "You won't be told again."

Depending on the men involved, it could become a bone-breaking fight, a converted new member, or the next morning a bunk would be found deserted because the previous owner headed for the tall timber.

A sash and door factory.

Industrial Worker.

LUMBER WORKERS
INDUSTRIAL UNION No. 120
VANCOUVER, B. C.

The Wobbly movement was not restricted to the United States. It was also prospering in the lumber regions of Canada. World War I had a profound effect upon social thinking. The old ways were dying—hard, but clearly dying. Bolshevicks announced the era of the workers was at hand as the old royal houses of Europe toppled. The Russian Revolution, which was as much a class struggle as the French Revolution, telegraphed its message all over the world. The men of great wealth feared this new, unpredictable trend which was being expressed by discontented soldiers returning home from war to high unemployment and to wages that were now lower than before the war. Tension was mounting implying another Russian Revolution could start anywhere.

A ban was passed on the importing of American socialist literature into Canada by the government. Any Canadian worker who became involved in union or socialist activities was blacklisted. Employers hired labor spies to work in the logging camps for the loggers—in opposition to the trend of the Americans, whose radical union philosophy started among the millworkers—were the most militant of the forestry workers. During the war, those Canadian union organizers who had opposed the draft into a "foreign war" were jailed. After the war they were jailed for other actions such as possessing illegal socialist material.

As history has proven, an idea whose time has come cannot be merely banned or jailed or beaten or murdered. The idea will persist, which it did in Canada when in 1919 the loggers organized themselves into the B.C. Loggers Union. Ernest E. Winch became secretary of the Union. He promptly set up camp committees and camp delegates. Loggers organized to walk out in Prince George, Princeton and Comox.

Despite the risk of being fired for being a "union man," loggers joined the union until it became the largest in B.C. The loggers combined with the sawmill workers, eventually creating a membership of 15,000 in what they called the Lumber Workers Industrial Union.

As in the United States, the Canadian labor leaders were accused of being foreign agitators being paid by Russian revolutionaries. Yet the union movement persisted, suffering from setbacks and rumors.

While wages did not come up to union expectations, working conditions improved as the union officials prodded for changes. Some companies needed little prodding for even management was changing. The old-time timber baron who maintained his company records on scribbled notes in his pocket was rapidly becoming an anachronism. Lumber companies were growing into giants which required new management techniques and especially better working relations to maintain production schedules.

In Canada the James Logging Company of Cowichan was such a leader as would be Weyerhaeuser Company in the United States. The resistance came from smaller timber operators who would disappear in the great worldwide depression of the 1930s. Their holdings would be bought by the large timber companies which had started to change on their own, listening to and even accepting union demands.

But for those few timber operators whose time in the sun was about thirty years, all change was resisted. In their resistance lives would be upset and destroyed. The labor struggle that ripped apart the northwest woods was caused by a small faction of lumber barons who would be destroyed by their own stubbornness. The cost for them, as for the militant union logger or millworker, would be high.

Jones Photography; Aberdeen, Washington.

A 60 foot beam taken from one tree.

Jones Photography; Aberdeen, Washington.

The blacksmiths were the mainstay of pioneer logging.

Lumber camp file room where saws were sharpened.

Logging camp cook samples the hearty fare.

Seven of the Centralia Defendents. From left to right, back row: Bert Bland, John Lamb, Britt Smith, James McInerhey. Left to right, front row: O.C. Bland, Roy Becker and Eugene Barnett.

18

Centralia Incident

Typically small town, it was closely knit, dependent upon the brickyards and lumber companies of the area. The people were of a like mind with like concerns—especially among the businessmen who frequented Centralia's Elks Club. There is a question as to whether the Citizens' Protective League, which had been created to rid the county of Bolsheviks, actually met that night for the purpose of planning a raid on the I.W.W. hall.

Thereupon hangs the question: Did a group of businessmen gather to make plans for an Armistice Day raid on the I.W.W. hall as they had a year before? Did these same men who were representatives of the lumber interests use rhetoric to enflame strongly patriotic men to be their dupes?

The I.W.W. through the years of their existence maintained that such a meeting was held. The Citizens' Protective League and Legionnaires said there was no such meeting.

Obviously, local I.W.W. officials believed that the meeting did indeed take place for the expressed purpose of not only raiding the hall but running every Wobbly member — in particular I.W.W. Secretary Britt Smith—out of the county, if not the state.

What happened once the news of the meeting spread among the citizenry is history.

Also typically small town, the gist of the meeting circulated. The local newspapers picked up a thread of the story advocating the raid, even naming the men involved in the committee. The "secret meeting" had become local gossip, discussed on street corners, over breakfast, in camps and mills. Everywhere people gathered they talked about the raid and the intent to drive the Wobblies out of town.

Craft organizations held meetings asking how they should deal with the possible threat. The main suggestion was that the loggers close down the hall and leave town until feelings calmed. The loggers refused.

The secretary, with the approval of the membership, printed a leaflet in an appeal for public sympathy and support. The problem with such printed public appeals is to get people to read them. The appeal was ignored.

Armistice Day dawned under rain heavy, gray clouds. A raw wind mixed with the mist. Streets gleamed under cold sunlight. Ignoring the weather, people went about their business which was getting the parade on the road.

The owner of the Roderick Hotel in which the I.W.W. hall was located, recalling what happened to the last union hall, feared for his property. He appealed to Police Chief A.C. Hughes for protection.

The police chief answered, "We'll do the best we can for you, but as far as the Wobblies are concerned they won't last fifteen minutes if the businessmen don't want any Wobblies in this town."

The parade was the usual mixture of local clubs, veterans of previous wars all wearing dress uniforms, Boy Scouts and an automobile of girls dressed in Red Cross uniforms. The schoolchildren who were to have marched in the parade did not appear. The parade gathered at the city park. Onlookers commented how quiet the marchers were. Another asked why the marchers were carrying coils of rope. The sharp-eyed might have noticed the Centralia Legionnaires were well armed with loaded weapons that ranged from a Colt .45 to a high-powered Savage rifle.

The line of march was from the city park to Third Street and Tower Avenue, then return. The I.W.W. hall was located between Third and Second.

Marching in the parade were 520 uniformed veterans. As they proceeded north the Centralia veterans were in the lead followed by the Chehalis Legionnaires, who in turn were followed by the Boy Scouts, women who had been involved in the war effort, and the Elks Club with its band. That arrangement arrested worries for the watchful Wobblies. With the veterans at the head, followed by boys and women there was little concern about the rumors, afterall.

As the parade trooped past the union hall, local citizens expectedly glanced toward the buildings. Yet the procession continued without incident.

At Third Avenue the parade halted turning with an about face. This switch placed the Chehalis and Centralia contingents at the rear. The remainder of the parade, now at the front, returned along the same route. One by one each group marched past the hall where members inside stood by windows and watched the parade. The Chehalis contingent trooped past the hall. Following them, the Centralia group halted with a harsh tromp of feet against the pavement, closing up ranks.

There were and still are as many versions concerning what happened after that as there were witnesses. Some spectators claimed the parade stopped so that the other units could catch up. Wobblies believed the Legion members had stopped in preparation to raid the hall. Wobblies swore that the Legionnaires fired upon them. The Legionnaires said the Wobblies fired upon them.

Witnesses said they heard a Legionnaire shout, "I will enter the hall if enough of you will follow and back me up!"

Dr Frank Bickford, a Legionnaire, gave evidence in a coroner's jury that the door of the I.W.W. hall was forced open by the Legionnaires before the shooting started.

Dr. Herbert Beli, however, said the rush on the hall and the rifle fire from the hall were simultaneous.

Four shots were said to have echoed from within. Rifles were said to have been also fired from locations on Seminary Hill and the Avalon Hotel—supposedly by stationed Wobblies.

Staggering away was the new commander of the Grant Hodge Post of the American Legion, Warren O. Grimm. The thirty-year old Centralia attorney, a graduate of the University of Washington, was asked if he was badly hurt.

"I don't think so," he said while stumbling toward an auto. He managed to reach the rear of a soft drink place where he was rushed to the hospital. He died shortly thereafter.

Dead among the Legionnaires were Arthur McElfresh, pharmacy manager and Ben Casagranda. Wounded were Emery Coleman, H.W. Eubanks, John Earl Watt and Eugene Pfitzer. Fortunately, no spectators were harmed.

Inside the hall there had been as much confusion as from the outside. Bert Faulkner, unarmed, only wanted to get out of the hall. His escape on the backstairs was cut short by men with rifles. They ordered him to raise his hands and come down. In the rush of events, he couldn't clearly recall what happened inside the hall, but he would never forget the ride to jail in an automobile. Or the businessman holding a piece of gas pipe while guarding him.

Remaining in the battered hall were Roy Becker, Mike Sheehan, Les McInerney, Tom Morgan, Britt Smith and Wesley Everest. Everest was armed with a forty-four automatic and a pocketful of cartridges. Like Faulkner, Everest opted for escape. Although a mob had surrounded the rear of the building, they were too confused in reorganizing to pay heed to the young man slipping through and climbing the fence. A shout went up, "there's one of those damn Wobblies."

Waving a smoking gun, Everest warned, "don't follow me and I won't shoot."

Everest raced down the alley. The mob welled after him, pushing down the fence under the mass weight. Someone held up a rope and yelled to get the union secretary. The pursuit of Everest probably saved the lives of the trapped loggers—certainly the life of Britt Smith.

Everest would pause long enough to clip off a few shots at the mob, scattering them. He continued running, loading his gun as he darted out of the alley. The mob regrouped in hot pursuit. In an open gateway Everest paused again to shoot back at the mob. Sprinting between two frame dwellings, he ran out into the street. The mob raced after the young logger, all shouting, waving ropes and occasionally firing a rifle. For all the shooting no one was hit.

The chase continued one and one-half miles to the Skookum-chuck River which was running high with winter rain and snow drain-off. Why Everest paused in the water only he knew. Perhaps the water was too high. Perhaps he couldn't swim.

He returned to the shore and the mob. Holding the hot gun, he faced the crowd demanding, "stand back. If there are bulls in the crowd, I'll submit to arrest. Otherwise, lay off me."

Certain Everest's ammunition was gone, they surged closer. Shooting from the hip, Everest clipped off four shots. A man called Hubbard who had been leading the mob rushed him when the gun jammed. Everest cleared the gun and fired two more bullets hitting the soldier. Hubbard continued coming. At point blank range, Everest pumped the trigger twice more. The soldier was killed.

Men surged around Everest who struck back with fists. They overpowered him, beating him, half killing him. Tying the logger, the mob dragged him through the streets to the city jail. Within a half block of the jail the mob grew more unruly. They all tried striking at Everest, fighting with one another for the chance. They kicked, struck with doubled fists and spat. A businessman ripped pieces of skin from Everest's face. A woman slapped him. A soldier forced his way through the crowd to swing the rifle butt into Everest's mouth, smashing teeth. Blood splattered. A rope was thrown around his neck with the shout of "Let's finish the job."

At the city jail, Everest was thrown into the bull pen. Locked in nearby cells were the men who had been arrested at the union hall. Outside the jail the mob milled restlessly, all shouting for a hanging.

As planned, the lights of Centralia went out at 7 p.m., casting the small town into darkness. Under the cover of night, two cars with high frog-like headlights roared through the streets to the jail. The waiting mob cheered.

From outside the door could be heard the policeman on duty calling out, "don't shoot, men. Here's your man." A door moaned open. Footsteps sounded in the dark. The men in the other cells, not able to see anything, heard a struggle in Everest's cell and the sound of blows. More footsteps with a dragging sound. A door closed with a slam. Outside came the sound of automobile motors grinding gears.

The lights came on again and Everest was gone.

When questioned at the inquest how the mob broke into jail, Jailer Robert Jackson said he had been in the rear of the jail with a special deputy, admitting that the barred door between the office and corridor had been left unlocked.

Outside, the remaining mob shouted they wanted the other Wobblies. Inside the jail, the arrested men were questioned individually while three cars headed out of town, toward a bridge. During the trip over the bumpy roads, someone had castrated Everest.

Up ahead, car lights danced over the steel bridge framework. One car crossed over, stopping as the second car braked at the middle of the bridge. Behind it stopped the third car. Men exited to patrol both approaches to the bridge.

The bleeding Everest was hauled out of the second car. A rope was fastened around a girder. A connecting noose dropped around his neck. Headlights from two of the cars played over the scene as the men lifted Everest over the side of the bridge. They let him go but his fingers dug into the bridge planking until one of the businessmen stomped on the struggling fingers. The logger dropped with a jerk on the rope which twisted from body convulsions. The rope swayed. Leaning over the railing, the men pulled up the battered body. Removing the rope they attached a longer rope. The lynching was repeated. The body was again hauled up for an even longer rope. Again the body was kicked over the edge to sway on the fifteen foot long rope. Later, the ropes from the hangings would be cut up and handed out as souvenirs.

Going to their cars, the lynchers fetched rifles. They riddled the body with volley after volley. Satisfied at long last, they drove away leaving the body to dangle from the bridge.

Someone unknown cut down the body which splashed into the river and floated on the current.

The problem of a body that had been mutilated, hanged and shot worried the men involved—it might fall into the wrong hands. A search party gathered. Locating the corpse, the men returned the body to the city jail as an object lesson. Everest's body was dumped in a cell occupied by two loggers who had been his close friends.

Four union men claimed Wesley Everest's body. They buried the young logger's remains, refusing to tell anyone the location of the grave.

Trial was set for January, 1920 in the Grays Harbor County Hall of Justice.

The I.W.W. sought the best legal advice available—George Vanderveer. Vanderveer had defended the I.W.W. in a famous Chicago case and had also been the defense counsel for those charged in the Everett case.

When the trial opened on February 7, 1920 it was receiving national news media coverage. Charged with first degree murder of William O. Grimm were I.W.W. members Britt Smith, Eugene Barnett, Ray Becker, Bert Bland, O.C. Bland, Bert Faulkner, John Lamb, James McInerney, Mike Sheehan, Loren Roberts and Elmer Stuart Smith. While Smith had not taken part in the incident, he was the I.W.W. attorney and was indicted for having "aided, abetted and counseled the I.W.W. on the commission of the crime charged."

In his opening statement to the jury George Vanderveer announced that the I.W.W., rather than the accused, were on trial in Montesano; that it was not only a case of whether or not the Wobbly members were justified in defending their hall, as Elmer Smith had instructed them, but also a question of whether or not the I.W.W. was going to be permitted a place in the American labor union scene.

Referring to the Centralia Legionnaires who had raided the hall, he said "Those men were only the dupes of the city's Protective League. That League had conspired to do violence to the I.W.W. by wrecking the hall and driving the members out of Centralia as had happened the year before."

In rebuttal, the prosecution countered that the I.W.W. had "deliberately fired on the parading legionnaires," and that the attack had been "planned several days."

At the end of the 33-day trial, Vanderveer gave a two-hour summation trying to impress upon the jury that the I.W.W. had fired their guns only to protect their property.

The case went to the jury.

The jury found Mike Sheehan and Elmer Smith not guilty. They found Loren Roberts insane. Eugene Barnett and John Lamb were guilty of third degree murder. O.C. Bland, Ray Beck, Bert Bland, and Britt Smith were found guilty of manslaughter. Bert Faulkner had been released earlier in the trial for lack of evidence. Because there was no crime that allowed third degree murder, Judge Wilson refused the verdict, ordering them to reconsider their findings.

Following deliberations, the jury returned that same evening with their final verdict: "We find the following accused guilty of second degree murder. Eugene Barnett, John Lamb, O.C. Bland, Bert Bland, Britt Smith, Ray Becker and James McInerney." The jury also asked for leniency. Instead, Judge Wilson sentenced each man to 25 to 40 years of hard labor.

The men who had lynched Wesley Everest were never brought to trial.

Some questions arise after the passage of sixty years.

Were the Legionnaires the innocent dupes of the Citizens' Protective Association which was formed in October 1919 for the purpose of driving the I.W.W. from town. It is known that members of the Elks, American Legion and Citizens Protective Association met at the Elks Lodge in Centralia...but for what reason?

Why was only one armed guard left at the jail the night Wesley Everest was lynched? How did the mob break so easily into the jail? What happened to the Centralia and Chehalis Police records of that infamous night? What ever happened to the weapon Everest supposedly used to shoot and kill Hubbard?

Was a raid planned by the Legion? If so, and according to an appeal made to the I.W.W. to the citizens of Centralia, why wasn't the hall defended from within instead of from a hotel and a hill almost one mile distant as the prosecution contended?

Why didn't the police provide some kind of protection to the I.W.W. hall considering that Police Chief Hughes was aware of the existence the Citizens' Protective Association and their expressed purpose? Hughes was quoted as saying "If the Legion starts toward the I.W.W. hall to raid it there is nothing the police can do to stop it."

An advertisement appeared on page one of the Centralia Chronicle on November 12, 1919 stating "KEEP OFF THE STREETS. Chief of Police Hughes asks all law-abiding citizens to keep off the streets tonight as the best means of preserving order." That night Wesley Everest was brutally hanged.

Why didn't the police intervene in the mob action which it obviously knew about?

Who threw the switch that turned off all the lights in Centralia on November 12, 1919?

Even after sixty years, the questions haunt Western Washington like insistent whispering ghosts. All the I.W.W. members involved in the Centralia Incident are dead. A few Legionnaires still live, still maintaining that the Wobblies fired upon armed, ex-soldiers.

Loggers who married were sometimes provided with company houses for their families. The women supplemented income by raising chickens (destined for the stew pot) and selling fresh eggs.

19

Wobbly Demands

Industrial Worker.

What did the Wobblies demand for the workers that caused them to be called radicals, bolsheviks—the Red Terror?

Listed below are some of the radical demands the Wobblies fought for and in part achieved. They were only partly successful for the bad publicity arising against the I.W.W. as a result of the Centralia Incident destroyed their effectiveness as an organization in the timber industry.

- Reduce the ten-hour work shift to eight hours.
- Increase wages to a minimum of $4.85 a day.
- Provide free transportation to the job (applied to the deep timber logging camps).
- Provide hiring on the job or from a union hall, eliminating buying a job from a job shark, also known as a man hunter.
- Allow workers to join a union without fear of loss of a job.

In the logging camps provide:
- A drying room for wet clothes.
- Shower facilities for the loggers.
- Porcelain wash basins instead of enamel dishes.
- Proper sanitary toilet facilities.
- Care and hospitalization for the injured *immediately* instead of waiting until the end of the shift.
- Abolition of the bindle.
- Clean mattresses and bedding furnished by the company.
- Abolition of double-tier bunks.
- Abolition of muzzle-loading (getting as many men into as small an area as possible to eliminate building more bunkhouses).
- No more than twelve men to a bunkhouse instead of the usual twenty to fifty.

For such "outrageous" demands men and women were beaten and/or murdered.

ALL "BINDLES" WILL BE BURNED ON MAY FIRST

MAY THE FIRST 1918

139

I.W.W. picnic, 1910.

20

Seattle General Strike

During the Great War, wages in the Pacific Northwest had been stabilized below the usual pay scale and frozen. Yet inflation continued to spiral prices upward as much as fifty percent.

Basically inflation was explained in this way: Food and supplies sent to a starving Europe resulted in shortages in the United States. The result was "higher prices."

Wages were less. Prices were out of sight. Employers were getting rich for there was no control on profits or interest rates.

The war coming to an end changed nothing as long as wages remained frozen. There had been war-time controls on the right to strike. With the Armistice came the release of such strike controls. Strike talk began immediately.

The strike had to come from an organization in the most effective quarter—the unions which represented shipyards where record numbers of ships for the war effort had been built.

Prior to the war the Metal Trades Council negotiated for pay increases for the shipyard workers. That authority during the war had been given to the Shipbuilding Labor Adjustment Board in Washington, D.C. With the war over, the Metal Trades Council sent a representative to the Shipbuilding Labor Adjustment Board to confer with the Macy Board and the Emergency Fleet Corporation. It was the representative's understanding he had been granted permission to negotiate directly with the shipyards as long as wage increases did not affect the price of shipping to the government. With this in mind, he returned to Seattle.

Somewhere along the line a misunderstanding, intentionally or not, had occurred.

As the Metal Trades Council sounded out the policy of a strike vote and the backing of other unions in the area, a telegram messenger boy delivered, by mistake, a telegram addressed to the Metal Trades Association to the Metal Trades Council instead. In the telegram from the Emergency Fleet Corporation to the Association was the information that if there was a wage increase, there would be no more steel for the Seattle shipyards.

This caused understandable consternation at the Council. Only one thing was certain—if the unions were pitted against the companies in a wage increase demand, they could expect no assistance from the government. They stood alone.

Strike talks continued while the government urged shipyards to resist labor's demand. The war was over. There was no longer a crushing need for ships.

On January 22, 1919, the Central Labor Council held a meeting attended by 110 local unions. By February 2 the discussion had narrowed down to representatives from three unions. A strike date had to be settled upon.

It was to be a very special strike—the first general strike of its kind in the nation. All unions in Seattle working closely together would shut down a city of 300,000. Such action posed special problems requiring a committee of Fifteen to deal with civic management such as: food for those unmarried workers who ate in restaurants, providing police, aiding the ill and elderly, taking care of garbage, keeping civil order and preventing rioting and looting.

The strike was viewed differently by the local businessmen. They darkly saw it as an enraged army of working men pouring into the streets; looting, killing, raping and burning. They expressed their fears to the newspapers which turned out copy voicing those views. Machine guns were stationed in banks. Probably the only happy businessman was the one selling guns. His weapon inventory was rapidly depleted by the wealthier upper classes who were certain they would be the first targets. Many businessmen and families departed hastily for California or for Portland, Oregon.

There was, the businessmen announced, clearly a revolution coming to Seattle by red-flag waving bolsheviks. As the Seattle newspapers complained about the Red insurgents, word spread across the nation. Eastern news reporters flocked to Seattle to see the first American revolution Russian-style.

In the rumors was lost the intended purpose of the strike. The unions were asking a wage increase to the level of wages before the war and preferably higher. The purpose of the strike wasn't revolution but the pay-increase demand was drowned in newspaper articles crying against unpatriotic unions.

The mayor swore in extra police. He also summoned help from the governor in Olympia, asking for the National Guard.

142

The president of the University of Washington did the mayor one better. He demanded the Secretary of War send in federal troops to protect American citizens from the Red Menace.

The educational system was so geared to orient students for college that those children of working class parents usually quit school by age fourteen. Then the boys would pick up lunch buckets and follow their fathers into the mills or woods. Those students attending universities were children of wealthier parents. The university students, raised in a different more affluent atmosphere than the children of working classes, knew only that their parents were packing up and leaving to avoid the revolution. At the universities students were paid to act as guards while wearing their ROTC uniforms. Many bragged of getting their first Bolshevik. When asked about the issues, few knew more than the newspaper reporting of a revolution. Few understood or cared about the union demands.

Wiser heads ruled at the unions' Committee of Fifteen as they appointed Labor Guards to send home any crowds of working men who might knot together on streets. However, no crowds of working men gathered.

At 10:00 a.m., February 6, 1919 when the strike began, the working men simply left their jobs and went home. Streetcars were in the barns. Trucks had been left in garages. The streets became empty as transportation ceased.

Silence.

The usual whirl of machines at mills and factories stopped. Electricity still worked. Water continued to course through pipes. All the vital life functions of a city continued.

Labor had set up around the city twelve kitchens to feed people. A meal could be had for twenty-five cents if a worker had a union card. For all others, thirty-five cents.

A special provision was granted by the Strike Committee to milk wagon drivers and laundry drivers to continue supplying hospitals, babies and invalids with services.

The I.W.W. struck in sympathy, offering their services to the patrolling Labor Guards. Mainly, the Wobblies kept a low profile.

A waiting silence enveloped the city. Army lorries patrolled the streets. Strategic corners were sandbagged into machine gun nests. The city took on the overtones of any army-occupied foreign country. Yet all was so quiet and orderly, the commander of the Federal troops began to look on the rumors as so much hot air. He wanted to pull out.

Yet rumors spread. Gossip insisted the city center was in flames. People had been massacred—wealthy people. Lenin and Trotsky had been seen in the city on their way back to Russia. The

Bolsheviks were winning. The government troops were winning.

Reporting it all in graphic details were the newspapers. Perhaps such wild stories could give colorful copy to the eastern newspapers, but the ones that could not be pardoned were the local newspapers that knew better. Local newspaper publishers and editors knew, allowing for patrols, the streets were deserted.

Unfortunately, the unions learned that on which they had based their assumption was wrong. They had thought ships were needed when, in fact, ships were not. Especially not by those in the Seattle shipyards. Shipyards in the gulf coast states, in California and on the east coast continued to operate. The government didn't care whether or not the Seattle shipyards provided one more ship. The strike, while not achieving its purpose, did teach unions that a truly effective strike had to be nationwide. This one was not.

The Strike Committee decided Saturday would be a good day to end the strike. However, the mayor said the wrong thing to the Committee: "End the strike or else."

Or else what? The Strike Committee was outraged, becoming stubborn.

By Monday unions scattered around the city began reporting back to work. That same Monday the General Strike Committee met, agreeing to resume the strike. As a united front they would end the strike at noon, Tuesday, February 11, 1919.

The five-day so-called Bolshevik Revolution ended setting an example for other strikes that quiet, orderliness, non-violence and teamwork could be effective under the right circumstances.

WHICH PAPER DO YOU SUPPORT?

The unions became so powerful and popular with a large segment of the working population that the lumber interests weren't quite certain what to do about the Seattle Strike. There had been, in their opinion, a revolution—a class struggle. All revolutions had prisoners. Someone who could be blamed for crimes. A wrong-doer was required. Of the 110 unions involved in the strike, all were too powerful to raid and throw the members in jail.

The I.W.W. had the bad timing to print a leaflet which contained a cartoon of a man kicking a fat little man representing capitalists into a coffin under the heading: Russia Did It.

That was Criminal Syndicalism.

Wobbly leaders were arrested. In a mock trial the leaflet was produced as evidence for starting a revolution in Seattle.

Many Wobblies jumped freight cars and hurriedly departed. Others were caught in a dragnet.

Yet try as the lumber interests might during the May 21 trial, even they failed. The prosecution couldn't provide enough evidence that the I.W.W. and socialists had intended to use the strike as a means for revolution. The first case was acquitted. Deciding it was nothing but a waste of money to continue with the trial, the prosecution requested the other thirty cases be dismissed.

The Seattle Strike and the printed leaflet was enough to increase raids on Wobbly halls throughout the state, to arrest Wobbly leaders and run them out of town.

Signboard from I.W.W. Head-quarters.

A fire fighter watches the advance of a forest fire and plans alternative means to keep it in check.

21

Fire

To the logger a fight was great sport, be it in saloon or picket line. There was only one fight that made him go cold with fear. That was the shout of "fire in the timber!"

Loggers develop a sixth sense about forest fires, especially when the humidity goes down and the temperatures rise. During July and August when the fire threat is the greatest, the woods are usually shut down. The forest is a waiting tender box. Those sensitive to the danger can feel the hackles rise on the back of their necks.

Conifer needles are like gasoline. As flame licks up a tree it explodes from the pitch and needles with a shrieking scream. The slash—the pile of brush, rejected trees, chips, bark, curls, logs—left in the aftermath of a logging show has the same explosive tendency as nitroglycerin. A spark can set it off. A campfire can smolder for days until in the quiet woods the sparks gather life and race along the forest floor to spread into an uncontrollable wave.

The Yacolt fires in September, 1902, are believed to have been caused by loggers' or settlers' fires that had been smoldering since May. The summer was dry. On September 9 a "devil wind" blew steadily from the eastern semi-desert. The wind whined down the Cascades and sucked moisture from the forest. Forest moss became brittle and flammable. Twigs snapped like gun shots. Plants wilted. Animals became quiet, panting heavily in bedded down areas of the forest. The forgotten fires began to awaken. Humidity dropped to a terrible low.

Only those in Douglas fir country can understand how a jungle containing one of the largest species of trees on earth can explode like gunpowder. For that is exactly what it does: Boom! No warning except that it has been too hot, and when it explodes there is no escape.

The woods blew up in 1902. One hundred and ten times in Washington and Oregon. The western portion of Washington was ablaze from the Columbia River to the Canadian border in an inferno that made the winds rise. Atmospheric pressure was affected. One fire alone devoured 250,000 acres of timber.

Ashes rained from a smoke-black sky. Portland, Oregon recorded wood ash piled as deep as one-half inch on the sidewalks and streets. In Seattle, citizens witnessed clouds of fire dancing in the sky.

People believed Mount Tacoma had erupted. Religious fanatics screamed the end of the world had come. So it did for thirty-five people.

The fires had started so quickly many could not escape. A smoky sky caused no worry in 1902. To clear a forest with fires was standard practice. Summer was always a time of smoke. Then, through a draw in the hills, would come a wall of fire that shot exploding fireballs. More fires were started. Like a hurricane, the fire advanced. Horses couldn't outrun the sheet of flames. People were found in the remains of homesteads and townships. All had tried to flee but the fire had rushed over them like molten lava.

The smoke and ashes blotted out a wan sun. Lanterns had to be used at twelve noon. Clark County became a massive inferno. Reports drifted in from the westernmost town of Hoquiam which huddled at bayside—Chehalis county[28] was ablaze, dark by day and lighted by fires at night. Ninety miles to the east in the capitol city of Olympia, located on a southern finger of Puget Sound, came news that business had ceased and lanterns had to be used during the day. In Chehalis, church bells summoned people to pray. Apocalypse. Revelations. Fires were reported as far east as Walla Walla where the wheat crop was destroyed. Enumclaw was threatened by the fire. In Astoria, Oregon girls in the Sanborn-Cutting Packing Company dropped on their knees at work and prayed as fires threatened the town from the east and south. A change in the wind saved Tillamook City, Oregon. In Eugene, Oregon the cinders were so thick that anything four blocks distant couldn't be seen.

Whole families disappeared. Towns swept up by the flames were never rebuilt. Even after seventy years scars remain in old dry snags. The land was rendered sterile by the heat.

The Yacolt Burn became a grim memory.

* * *

August 14, 1933, the Tillamook, Oregon fire.

Temperatures climbed to 100 degrees with a drop in humidity as the old nemesis, the devil wind, blew from the east. At a logging camp, a spark danced from the friction of a steel logging cable rubbing on a cedar log. The spark tumbled into fire-fuel—slash— and smoked into flame. The crew grabbed shovels, axes, fire fighting equipment but the fire spread, rippled through debris and grew to burn up four centuries of trees.

A crew of Civilian Conservation Corps joined the hundreds of men fighting the fire.

On August 19, the wind died down. For a while they thought they might rest but on August 20 the wind rose rapidly. The flames roared through the fire lines and advanced two hundred feet gaining speed. The CCC camps were evacuated. Within seconds the fire raged through.

On August 20-21, 1919, flames gusted through northeastern Washington, Northern Idaho and Montana. Eight billion board feet of timber was destroyed. Of the eight-five people killed in the fire and resulting hurricane winds, seventy-two were firefighters.

* * *

For ten days the fires roared, destroying 311,000 acres—12 billion board feet. In one twenty-four hour span the winds from the exploding, flaming trees whirled upward into a maelstrom of hurricane proportions that threw out burning debris. A strong easterly wind blew fire ash and burned chunks of wood on the decks of ships 500 miles at sea. Rising to altitude of 40,000 feet billowing brownish-gray clouds blotted out the sun. One hundred miles to the north in Portland, a weak orange drab sun peered through the haze of smoke and ash.

A total of 27,000 of the 311,000 acres were burned within twenty-four hours.

The Tillamook fire became known simply as the "Big Burn." For miles nothing existed except soot, ashes, and naked black sticks that had once been trees.

As one logger-firefighter said, "Fire is a goddamn four-letter word."

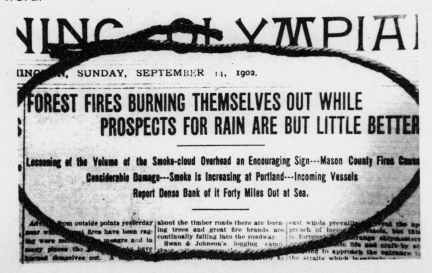

This Evening Olympian headline reflects the impact of the forest fires in the early 1900's.

22

The Fiddler Died

One day the logger looked around him. By the dynamitin' ol' so-and-so, if civilization hadn't caught up with him again. But this time he was smack up against the Pacific Ocean. There was no more hump into which to axe daylight in the swamp.

But he was a different kind of logger now. Unlike the logger of old, he had married and settled down in a comfortable home. The mortgage was in his name, no longer a company shack. He paid taxes. It was his father who had fought for the unions. All that was remembered of the wild old days were the memories and stories of old men. There were no more six months in deep timber. The town skidroads where loggers had had their blow-outs disappeared or have been reduced to a plight of flophouses and pan-handling winos.

Civilization certainly did finish off the fist-pounding, rib-stomping, foul-mouthed, strong-smelling logger of the turn of the century.

They don't kill the fiddler anymore. No, it ain't done that way no more.

British Columbia Recalled
by Derek Pethick and Susan Im Baumgarten
Hancock House Publishers, Ltd.
1974

The Centralia Case;
Three Views of the Armistice Day Tragedy at
Centralia, Washington
The Centralia Conspiracy by Ralph Chaplin
Centralia—Tragedy and Trial by Ben Hur Lampman
The Centralia Case: A Joint Report
De Capo Press
1971

Chechacos All
by A Committee of the Skagit County Historical
Society, Margret Willis, Editor
Mount Vernon, WA
1973

The Dry Years: Prohibition and
Social Change in Washington
by Norman Clark
University of Washington Press
1965

Famous Northwest Manhunts and Murders
by Hollis Fultz
Elma Chronicle Printing Press
1955

Glory Days of Logging
by Ralph W. Andrews
Superior Publishing
1974 (reprint)

A History of Lumbering in Maine 1861-1960
by David C. Smith
University of Maine Press
1972

The History of the Northern Interior of British Columbia
by A.G. Morice
Ye Galleon Press
Fairfield, WA, 1971

History of the White Pine Industry in Minnesota
by Angnes M. Larson
University of Minnesota Press
1949

Land of Giants
by David Lavender
Doubleday & Company, Inc.
1956-1958

Logger Life, Love and Laughter
by Art Mackey
Loggers World, Inc.
Chehalis, Washington

Lumbering Songs from the Northern Woods
by Edith Fowke
The University of Texas Press
Austin and London
1970

The Last Wilderness
by Murray Morgan
Viking Press
1955

Milltown
by Norman H. Clark
University of Washington Press
1970

Mills and Markets
by Thomas R. Cox
University of Washington Press
1974

Bibliography

Northwest Gateway
by Archie Binns
Binfords & Mort, Publishers
1941

Pioneer Days in British Columbia, Volumes I and II
A selection of historical articles from
BC Outdoors Magazine
1973

Roaring Land
by Archie Binns
R.M. McBride
1942

Skidroad
by Murray Morgan
Viking, 1955
revised edition published by Ballantine Books, 1971

Sons of the Profits, or,
There's No Business Like Grow Business,
The Seattle Story 1851-1901
by Bill Speidel
Nettle Creek Publishing Company
1967

This was Logging
by Ralph W. Andrews
Superior Publishing
1968

Timber
by A.K. Larssen and Ralph W. Andrews
Superior Publishing
1978

Timber! The Way of Life in the Lumber Camps
by James Stevens
Row, Peterson & Company
1942

Timber: History of the Forest Industry in B.C.
by G.W. Taylor
J.J. Douglas, Ltd, Vancouver
1975

Washington, West of the Cascades
Volumes I, II, III
by Herbert Hunt and Floyd C. Taylor
S.J. Clarke Publishing Company
1917

The Way of the Logger
by Paul Petteto
Loggers World, Inc.
Chehalis, Washington
1970

Vancouver Island and British Columbia
by Mathew MacFie
Longman, Green, Longman, Roberts
& Green of London
1865

Glossary

The following is a list of common logging expressions with a brief definition. Some expressions could not be printed. Many of the old-time logging terms have become a vital part of the American language.

A

A day late—before union halls were established, loggers gained jobs from employment sharks. This was the sharks' remark when no work was available.

A dollar short—again the employment sharks' statement when the logger had no money to pay the employment fee.

A raft of—a raft of logs originally, coming to mean a lot of anything.

A shot in the brush—slashing a railroad into deep timber.

Abortion—odd machinery. A swear word to use on stubborn equipment.

According to Hoyle in the book of snags—The Authority. Often unwritten rules stressing how something should be done as explained by old timers to greenies.

Accordion—ripples or rough notching across log end, caused by poor bucking.

Ace in the hole—loggers love poker, too.

Admiralty shackle—used in skyline logging. Heavy shackle at tail tree linking skyline to stub line.

Aerial roading—Can mean skyline haul or hauling by tramway.

After-cut—back cut. Final cut in falling tree.

Agitator—troublemaker.

Alabama wool—cotton underwear or clothing in general.

Aladdin—gas mantle lamp used in camp bunk houses.

Alibi day—during camp payday loggers suddenly developed a variety of ills, such as toothache, that required going to town. Such as expression "getting my teeth fixed."

Alky—sometimes called moonshine. Anything alcohol, reputedly high quality that could be drank.

American—depending on usage could be railroad log loader. More often a rod locie (locomotive), either saddle bag (or saddle tank) or with usual tender.

Artist—a man skillful at his job.

Ask for time—Take a walk. Quitting.

Asphalt logger—logger preferring town to camp. Sometimes long on talk in town, short on work in camp.

Ax'er—cut anything loose.

Ax handle party—A fight using ax handles or anything else wooden.

Axle grease—butter.

B

Back country—Anything distant, usually uncut timber.

Back cut—After cut.

Back drum—Donkey drum closest to the boiler on steam rig. Sometimes next to engine on gas or diesel rig.

Back forty—Almost as far away as the back country. The ideal logging show that is somehow never found.

Back his play—back up a man.

Back to camp—Following a strike or a shut down, to go back to work.

Backin' the breeze—someone so full of talk he can make the wind blow backward.

Backfire—Setting fire in front of a coming forest fire. Best left to the experts.

Backs up to the window for his paycheck—Someone who does so little work he's embarrassed to take pay.

Bait—good meal. Sometimes a block used in leverage for prying.

Bait can—lunch bucket.

Bald-headed—anything bare from tires to hair. Including doing a job by brute strength and no savvy.

Baldwin—rod engine.

Balloon—logger's bindle.

Balloon it—pack and leave camp.

Banana belt—usually a mild, even warm winter. More rare, an easy show.

Bar toad—Someone who goes into a saloon and squats there the whole time, almost like a toad on a lily pad.

Barb wire deal—tough problem or situation.

Barefoot—lacking calks.

Bark—the outside of anything such as on a log or tree. To cut bark. Noise made by a steam engine. To slice off skin on knuckles or shins.

Boiling dishwater—To determine how cold the weather is, throw boiling dishwater outside. If it freezes before hitting ground, it's cold.

Bone butcher—company doctor.

Bow and arrow—an Indian.

Bow-back—stooped over, usually permanently from working too long in the woods.

Bow his back—refuse to do a job.

Boy—any male not ready for wheel chair.

Brainless wonder—someone who thinks he knows more than he does.

Brush ape—logger.

Bucked—Trees felled from which logs are cut up.

Bucker—man who cuts felled trees.

Buckskin—peeled log.

Buckwheat show—sometimes easy logging, usually logging show made up of greenies.

Buckwheater—newcomer to woods.

Bug chaser—Vermin remover. Popular man in lice-ridden logging camps.

Bull—full of.

Bull cook—besides a cook, also does odd jobs.

Bull head—Contrary.

Bull of the woods—Could be one tough man in camp, or the boss, or a top hand.

Bull pen—pen where unsorted logs are dumped. Place where men gather or sleep. Recreation room in modern camps.

Bump—seniority system of taking job from man with less time on job.

Bunch the job—quitting without warning.

Bunk-bound—logger who prefers to stay in bed.

Bunkhouse fable—often impossible to believe stories about last trip to town.

Bushwhacker—man who will turn on you.

C

Cabin fever—alone so long one starts talking to himself. Deep timber sickness that afflicted entire crews.

Cable road—incline logging railroad.

Caked up—drunk on extracts meant for baked cakes.

Camp inspector—logger who moves rapidly from one camp to another. Moves even faster than a short-stake man.

Camp lawyer—either logger or flunky who has to argue about everything.

Camp louse—camp roustabout.

Camp push—local boss.

Camp robber—Man always bumming a lunch, will even grab any food left unattended. A Canada jay.

Can opener artist—a poor cook, only slightly better than a belly robber.

Candy—either fancy or well-rigged.

Candy kid—the boss's fair-haired boy.

Candy side—the best logging show possible.

Canned cow—tinned milk.

Canned heat—Disgusting, poisonous drink refined by squeezing gelatinized alcohol through a sock. Especially a used sock.

Chicken—Anything between a robin and an eagle was a chicken.

Chicken crap outfit—crummy logging show.

China boy—Chinese logger.

China house—cookshack and bunkhouse used by Chinese loggers. The Chinese did their own cooking, worked on separate timber and did not mingle with other loggers.

Chinook—a dialect made up of various Indian words from various tribes, a little French, a little English, a lot of cussing. The North Coast Indians simply didn't want to be bothered learning English, so they didn't. They let the white man figure it out for himself.

Cookee—kitchen helper.

Cookhouse cost—bookkeeping loss when serving decent meals below cost to keep loggers contented.

Cookie pusher—biscuit shooter. A waitress.

Copenhagen—chewing tobacco. Snoose.

Corks—how loggers saw calks.

Cosmopolis flush—a four-card flush in a poker. Cosmopolis, a town once frequented by loggers "going down to splash," is a sister city to Aberdeen and Hoquiam in Washington.

Cotton picker—a dark-skinned logger, or simply any dark complexed logger.

Cougar juice—Kerosene used for cleaning pitching off gummed saw teeth. Also whiskey strong enough to melt glass.

Cougar milk—home brew aged long enough to add bark to a man's head.

Crazy as an outhouse rat—could anything be crazier?

Cream—the best logging show; the best of anything.

Cremated—overcooked piece of meat.

Crock—whiskey bottle.

Crooked elbow—caused by leaning against too many saloon bars.

Crosscut—saw used in falling and hand bucking.

Crown—branches of a standing, live tree.

Cruise—inventory standing timber.

Cruiser—a timber estimator, or a logger looking for trouble.

D

Dashboards—farmers who worked as part-time loggers. So named because of their bib overalls.

Dentist—saw filer. One working on crosscut saws.

Devil dust—false smoke causing worry about forest fire.

Devil wind—forest fire wind, see "Fire in the Timber."

Devil's club—nasty plant in damp Northwest woods, has sharp spines that leave a lingering memory.

Dinkey—small locie.

Dirty old double-dyped, two-tonsiled, swivel-nose, knock-kneed, blue-headed, etc.,etc.,etc.—cussing.

Dog-robber—camp cook who feeds everything to loggers, has nothing left for dog.

Dolbeer—original donkey engine.

Down—temporary shut down.

Down timber—timber usually felled by a wind storm.

Drag'er—quitting job.

Drag day—day of month when man can draw his wages in advance of due day.

Draw day—pay day.

Draw your time—you're fired.

Drop seat—union suit underwear.

E

Easy as falling off a log—fall off a log and see how easy it can be, and painful.

Eats like a shagpoke—has an appetite bigger than Erickson's bar.

Eye—loop spliced into end of wire rope.

F

Faller—a man who cuts down trees.

Family camp—logging camp with houses for families.

Family show—logging operation run by an old man and his sons.

Fan dodge—dysentery.

Feather merchant—small logger.

Fell so far the bluebirds built a nest on him afore he landed—fall off a tall spar tree.

Felled—trees and shangs that have been cut down.

Felled and bucked—down trees bucked up ready for yarding.

Figure head—bookkeeper.

Fink—stool pigeon, company guard, private detective, double crosser. When Wobblies said it, they had reason and they were ready to fight the so-and-so with axe handles.

Fire bug—crazy person who sets fires.

Fire danger—time of good working weather and often bad fire weather. Usually calls for shutdown of logging operations.

Fire season—May to October when fire danger is at its height.

Fish eyes—poorly cooked tapioca.

Fixer—camp blacksmith.

Flea-bag—flop house, lice-occupied hotel.

Flunkie—table waiter, dishwasher.

Fly bread—raisin bread.

Folded up his face—stop talking.

G

Gall stones—hard beans, pits in cherry pie.

Galloping goose—any small steam or diesel locie not running smoothly.

Geared engine—Shay, Heisler or Climax locomotive.

Get your time—you're fired.

Gingered up—drunk on Jamaica ginger.

Give 'er snoose—feed in the power.

Go down the pike—quit the job.

Go down the road—quit or fired.

Go fishing—either to lay off or go on strike.

Go to town—get paid and head for town.

Goop—globby, sticky, smelly stuff.

Got 'er made—made a stake. Job well done.

Got flies on it—no good.

Grubpile—a call to eat.

Gunny sack show—haywire operation.

Gunny sack—haywire.

Gunpowder—black pepper.

Gut heater—whiskey.

Gut-shot—ulcer or other serious stomach trouble.

Gyppo—small logging operator who does contract work.

Gypsy—combination locie and donkey with two horizontal spools mounted on engine where pilot should be.

H

Hand shoes—gloves.

Hang an ax—put a handle in an ax.

Hang tough tit—stick to a decision.

Harbor (The)—Grays Harbor, Washington. Where most of the logging camps were.

Hardtack—Swedish flat bread. Any stale, stale bread.

Hardtack outfit—Operations that sets a poor table.

Has his tail up—not done in by hard luck.

Hash-house—cook house. Restaurant.

Hash-rassler—Flunky, cookee or waitress.

Haulback—line that returns the chokers to the woods after a turn of logs has been pulled in.

Haywire—anything broken that is fixed with haywire. Nothing works.

Haywire job—do anything the cheapest possible way. Taking chances.

Hermit—logger who prefers to work alone.

He's on the reservation—a logger fond of Indian women.

Hibernate—quit the woods and hole up for the winter.

Hid like a mouse in a bale of oakum—a very whiskery man.

Highball—do everything in a major hurry.

High climber—logger who climbs and tops tree to be used as a spar.

High pockets—a tall man.

High-tail—move as rapidly as a deer.

Hooker, hooktender—foreman of a yarding crew.

Hooktender's home—state mental hospital.

Hoosier—a greenhorn in the woods. One manages to foul up.

Hoosier up—to pull pranks on a greenie. Among Wobblies, to slow down work production rather than strike.

Hoot-nanny—small device holding crosscut saw while sawing log from underneath.

Horse blankets—flapjacks. Or heavy black underwear which is never washed and smells like a horse.

Hotcakes are too round—an excuse for quitting a job. A poor excuse is better than no excuse.

Hughie—a name for God.

Hump—hill.

Humped up like a chicken in a rainstorm—a cold, wet logger.

Hung up—stuck.

I

I.W.A.—International Woodworkers of America, the C. 10. loggers' union.

I.W.W.—International Workers of the World. Wobblies.

If you know, you don't go hungry—meaning a good logger could always find work.

I'll cut my suspenders and go straight up—one mad logger.

In a jam—log jam. Trouble.

In the boondocks—deep timber.

In the sock—money put away.

Independent logger—a logger who sells his logs on the open market, not under contract.

J

Jack up—bawl out a worker.

Jakey—Jamaica ginger flavoring. Especially favored during the Prohibition.

Jawbone—talk. Verbal contract.

Job shark—employment agent.

Join the birds—to get off moving equipment in great haste because of danger.

Jump—movement of tree when falling from stump.

Jungle—thicket. Skidroad. Deep timber.

Juniper juice—gin.

K

King pin—center pin on which truck swivels. Head man.

King snipe—boss of track laying crew.

Kitchen mechanic—sometimes a cook, more often a dishwasher.

Knock off his hames—fire a man.

Knock out the bud—cut off the tree top for use as a spar.

Knothead—man as useless as a knot in a board.

L

L.S.W.U.—The Lumber and Sawmill Workers Union, and American Federation of Labor union in chiefly mills.

Lay off—shut down an operation.

Learnt by hand—on the job experience, not from a book.

Light a fuse—cause trouble.

Like a duck going to water—easy job, running smooth.

Like a handful of ants—everything in confusion.

Little bull—foreman either too young or lacking experience. Not yet a bull of the woods. Not respected by his men.

Little casino—hanger-on.

Liver pads—flapjacks.

Locie—logging locomotive. Also called a hog.

Log brand—To prevent rustling, ownership marks were hammered in log butt ends.

Log deck—or cold deck. Where logs are brought to deck of mill for sawing.

Logger's can opener—an ax.

Logger's smallpox—what a man looked like after being stomped on by calkboots.

Long Johns—long handled underwear.

Looked like a widow woman's ranch run on shares—poorly maintained operation.

Looking at the daisies from the root end—dead and buried.

Looking for a stretcher ride—what could come of horseplay and other stupid chances.

M

M—one thousand board feet.

Macaroni—long curls of sawdust.

Mad as a bear with a sore tail—Leave that contrary man alone.

Madder'n a polluted pole cat—Real mad, but not quite as bad as bear with sore tail.

Mail order woman—wife obtained through matrimonial bureau.

Make 'er pay—to be successful in anything.

Man catcher—employment agent. Usually found hanging around pool hall. Also called man getter, man grabber and less genteel handles.

Man shark—employment agent who took a logger's fee and sent him to a camp where there was no job.

Measure—loggers preferred to measure things by the size of Erickson's bar. Lengths were determined by ax handles. Wide things compared to a school ma'am's lap. Small things according to plugs of Star tobacco.

Mix me up a walk—quitting and wants paycheck. Also said "make 'er out," also said Counting the Ties when a man had to walk the railroad track back into town from deep timber.

Monthly insult—paycheck.

Mooch—panhandle.

Mud—coffee.

Mukluks—any soft, uncalked boots or shoes.

Mulligan—stew brought into the woods for the noontime meal.

Mulligan mixer—camp cook.

Muzzle loader—anything loaded or entered from the head end. Especially a bunk.

N

Never sweat—a lazy man.

Night rabbit—man running from law.

No-bill—non-union man.

No-blanket camp—meaning loggers supplied their own blankets.

No more teeth than an old hoss turned out to pasture—shoes without calks.

North Sea piano—concertina played by a Scandinavian logger.

Nosebag show—camp where midday meal was taken to the woods in lunch buckets.

O

Oakie—native of Oklahoma.

Off his feed—a sick man.

Off the reservation—can't understand the local customs.

Oklahoma hooktender—an inferior whistle punk.

On the ball—highball outfit. Good worker.

On the boat—logger going to a coastal logging camp that could be reached only by boat.

On the peck—short-tempered.

On the prod—Mad. Or anxious to get work done.

On the prowl—looking for trouble. Quitting.

On the rods—riding trains in search of job.

On the skids—slipping.

On the tramp—fired. No good.

One-choker show—tough outfit.

One-donkey show—very small operation.

Out in the tules—really back in the boondocks.

Outlaw—bad man. Machine which had killed a man. A dangerous tree.

Overland trout—bacon.

P

P.V.—after a trip to town, this remedy was much sought after.

Pack—bindle, personal gear.

Pack a card—union man.

Pack rat—besides the obvious rat, a man who collects anything.

Pack the balloon—take bindle and leave camp.

Pack the rigging—Wobbly term. To carry union and Wobbly publications.

Panther juice—a formidable drink

Panther sweat—any formidable drink

Pants rabbits—parasites.

Pass the 44's—Pass the beans.

Pavement pusher—a logger looking for a job from employment offices.

Pay cheater—company timekeeper.

Peasouper—because the French Canadians had a taste for pea souper they became known as peasoupers.

Peavey—long, stout handled tool with a spike used for rolling logs.

Pie in the sky—paradise, usually unobtainable.

Q

Q—Chinese logger, so named because of their long queues.

Queen's palace—separate bunkhouse for female cookhouse employees.

Quick like a cow—clumsy, two-left feet.

Quick like a squirrel—fast feet.

Quick step—dysentery.

R

Raft—usually, logs gathered in booms for river transport to mill.

Ramrod—foreman.

R'ar of snoose—gob of snoose. There was an art to chewing which separated the dudes from the real loggers.

Red card—Wobbly membership card.

Rod engine—standard steam engine.

Roll out or roll up—get to work or roll up your blanket.

Roll your blanket—you're fired.

Rolled—robbed while drunk.

Route—total length of time at camp; long route meaning long-time employment on one job.

Run your face—seek credit at company store.

S

S.O.S.—creamed beef.

Saddle blanket—a tough flapjack.

Saving himself work—said of a logger who marries a widow with a large brood.

Scandinavian dynamite—snoose.

School's out—hell to pay.

Scissor bill—non-union worker.

Seam squirrel—body louse.

T

Tacoma—steam donkey engine.

Tailor made—logging boots made to order.

'Tain't weather, it's a disease—long time of bad weather.

Take five—time for brief rest.

Talking to his blankets—man leaving in a hurry with his bindle to avoid being fired.

Tall uncut—virgin timber.

Tangle with a buzz saw—be on the worse end of a fight.

Tar—really bad coffee.

Tarp—a flapjack like canvas.

The baby is born—job is done.

The big bear walks—something is going to happen. Or time to eat.

The more you stir it the more it stinks—let it be or it'll get worse.

Thinks he throws two shadows—high opinion of himself.

Throw the bedroll in the bunkhouse—work at a logging show.

Throw up—quit.

Tick—so lazy the man can't work.

Tie a can on—fire someone.

Tiger crap—sticky mud.

W

Wakes up like a goose in a new world every morning—brains function like a goose.

Walk the bugs to death—turn shirt inside out so lice must walk to front to get in.

Walkaway Burns—a man who quit for no reason.

Walking appetite—can never get enough to eat.

Wangan—where camp stores are kept, and charges goods against payroll; river drivers camp.

War club—any wooden handle whether axe or peavey that can be used in a fight.

War department—a wife.

War whoops—Indians.

Warp it to him—make it rough for a man.

Water and chalk—inferior milk.

These few expressions are among the most colorful. Some have become a part of modern language. The more technical definitions were not included. To know more about the language of the loggers, a comprehensive dictionary is needed. The Oregon Historical Society has published such a dictionary called "Woods Words." The 219-page book written by Dean Walter R. McCulloch, School of Forestry, Oregon State College, thoroughly compiles the technical, the unusual and the expressive loggers' reflections. The soft-cover book is available for $3.25 plus handling from the Oregon Historical Society, Portland, Oregon.

Index

PRINTED IN CANADA